Fresh Ways with
Salads

TIME LIFE BOOKS

COVER
Wild strawberries add a surprise hint of sweetness to a medley of mild and bitter greens (recipe, page 18). The curly endive, Batavian endive, red oakleaf lettuce and radicchio in this salad offer vitamins and minerals but barely register on the calorie count.

TIME-LIFE BOOKS

EUROPEAN EDITOR: Ellen Phillips
Design Director: Ed Skyner
Director of Editorial Resources: Gillian Moore
Chief Sub-Editor: Ilse Gray

Correspondents: Elizabeth Kraemer-Singh (Bonn); Maria Vincenza Aloisi (Paris); Ann Natanson (Rome).

LOST CIVILIZATIONS
HOW THINGS WORK
SYSTEM EARTH
LIBRARY OF CURIOUS AND UNUSUAL FACTS
BUILDING BLOCKS
A CHILD'S FIRST LIBRARY OF LEARNING
VOYAGE THROUGH THE UNIVERSE
THE THIRD REICH
MYSTERIES OF THE UNKNOWN
TIME-LIFE HISTORY OF THE WORLD
FITNESS, HEALTH AND NUTRITION
HEALTHY HOME COOKING
UNDERSTANDING COMPUTERS
THE ENCHANTED WORLD
LIBRARY OF NATIONS
PLANET EARTH
THE GOOD COOK
THE WORLD'S WILD PLACES

HEALTHY HOME COOKING

SERIES DIRECTOR: Dale M. Brown
Deputy Editor: Barbara Fleming
Series Administrator: Elise Ritter Gibson
Designer: Herbert H. Quarmby
Picture Editor: Sally Collins
Photographer: Renée Comet
Text Editor: Allan Fallow
Editorial Assistant: Rebecca C. Christofferson

Editorial Staff for *Fresh Ways with Salads:*
Book Manager: Andrea E. Reynolds
Assistant Picture Editor: Scarlet Cheng
Researcher/Writer: Susan Stuck
Writer: Margery A. duMond
Copy Co-ordinators: Elizabeth Graham, Ruth Baja Williams
Picture Co-ordinator: Linda Yates
Photographer's Assistant: Rina M. Ganassa

European Edition:
Designer: Lynne Brown
Sub-Editor: Wendy Gibbons
Production Co-ordinator: Maureen Kelly
Production Assistant: Deborah Fulham

THE COOKS

ADAM DE VITO began his cooking apprenticeship when he was only 14. He has worked at Le Pavillon restaurant in Washington, D.C., taught with cookery author Madeleine Kamman, and conducted classes at L'Académie de Cuisine in Maryland.

HENRY GROSSI was awarded a Grand Diplôme at the École de Cuisine La Varenne in Paris. He then served as the school's assistant director and as its North American business and publications co-ordinator

JOHN T. SHAFFER is a graduate of The Culinary Institute of America at Hyde Park, New York. He has had a broad experience as a chef, including five years at The Four Seasons Hotel in Washington, D.C.

CONSULTANTS

CAROL CUTLER is the author of many cookery books. During the 12 years she lived in France, she studied at the Cordon Bleu and the École des Trois Gourmandes, as well as with private chefs. She is a member of the Cercle des Gourmettes and a charter member and past president of Les Dames d'Escoffier.

NORMA MACMILLAN has written several cookery books and edited many others. She has worked on various cookery publications, including *Grand Diplôme* and *Supercook*. She lives and works in London.

PAT ALBUREY is a home economist with a wide experience of preparing foods for photography, teaching cookery and creating recipes. She has contributed to a number of cookery books and was the studio consultant for the Time-Life series *The Good Cook*.

SANDRA CONRAD STRAUSS is president of Consumer Concepts, an American consulting firm specializing in consumer education about fresh produce. She is the author of *Fancy Fruits and Extraordinary Vegetables*, a cookery book that features some of the more unfamiliar and unusual foods available today.

NUTRITION CONSULTANTS

JANET TENNEY has been involved in nutrition and consumer affairs since she received her master's degree in human nutrition from Columbia University. She is the manager for developing and implementing nutritional programmes for a major chain of supermarkets.

PATRICIA JUDD trained as a dietician and worked in hospital practice before returning to university to obtain her MSc and PhD degrees. For the last 10 years she has lectured in Nutrition and Dietetics at London University.

Nutritional analyses for *Fresh Ways with Salads* were derived from Practorcare's Nutriplanner System and other current data.

This volume is one of a series of illustrated cookery books that emphasize the preparation of healthy dishes for today's weight-conscious, nutrition-minded eaters.

Fresh Ways with Salads

BY

THE EDITORS OF TIME-LIFE BOOKS

Contents

Alfalfa Sprouts and Red Onion Salad

Midsummer Melon Salad with Almond Oil

Lobster Salad with Sweet Peppers and Coriander

Salad's Special Magic

What fresher, more inviting food is there than salad? It seems to radiate good health, and so it should: the tenderest of greens, the crunchiest of roots, the leanest of meats and poultry, the most nutritious seafood, the most wholesome of grains, beans and pasta are among its raw materials. And, as if this in itself were not advertisement enough of salad's virtues, it is a dish than need not be fussed over, and one that can often be made quickly.

A salad can be the most varied of dishes. It may be as simple as a bowl of lettuce tossed with a light vinaigrette, or a more complex composition of meats and vegetables that might serve as a meal. Its elements can be either raw or cooked, or a mixture of the two, and it can be served chilled, at room temperature, or even warm.

This book alone contains enough salads — 123 in all — to suit any appetite; what is more, they have been judiciously created to take into account today's need for lighter, healthier eating. For example, the cold lobster with sweet peppers and coriander in a citrus vinaigrette on page 104 adds up to only 190 calories a serving; the asparagus salad with Jerusalem artichokes on page 21 comes to about 45 calories per portion.

Even the ancient Greeks knew that salad was healthy; they held it to be a food of the gods. In Shakespearean England, so-called fountains of youth, assembled from the first tender herbs and lettuces of spring, were eagerly consumed as antidotes to the grim winter diet. The great French gastronome Brillat-Savarin summed it up nicely: "Salad refreshes without weakening and comforts without irritating," he wrote in 1825, "and it makes us younger."

Whether truly rejuvenating or not, salad is, with its endless choice of ingredients, a bountiful source of minerals, vitamins and other nutrients. And when it is dressed carefully, salad will be low in fat as well, and thus in calories. The fact that most types of lettuce are between 90 and 95 per cent water is bound to give some people reason to cheer.

Salads made with grains, dried beans or pasta are loaded with complex carbohydrates — the main source of energy for the human body — and protein. Dried beans offer a particularly generous supply of fibre and protein; but for all their protein to be utilized by the body, they must be coupled with other foods that offer complementary proteins. As luck would have it, many of these are the very ingredients of successful modern salads — wheat, rice, meat and dairy products, to list a few. Thus the black bean and rice salad with red and green pepper strips on page 76 is not just a delicious meal; it is a highly nutritious one, supplying about a third of the body's daily protein needs.

As this book makes patently clear, salad need never be the same from one meal to the next. The salad-maker today is aided greatly by the presence of once-exotic ingredients in the supermarket, including a wider variety of fresh herbs.

The range of available vinegars and salad oils has increased as well, along with the number of different prepared mustards. Wine, tarragon, balsamic and Chinese black vinegars lend a new liveliness to salad dressings, as do oils as diverse as walnut, almond and dark sesame.

Freshness above all

Our salad bounty is enhanced still further by the seasonal appearance of several delightful ingredients. Asparagus might well stand as the emblem of spring; tomatoes plump and red from basking in the sun evoke summer, as does golden sweetcorn, its kernels swollen with sweet juice. Cabbages and root vegetables show up abundantly in autumn. Many of the recipes in this volume would greatly benefit from the inclusion of vegetables picked at their peak of ripeness and flavour. Faster, improved transport and distribution, as well as local produce stalls in street markets, make this possible by putting an array of perfectly ripened ingredients at the salad-maker's disposal.

Fruit has played a time-honoured role in many salads. A greater availability of seasonal produce and an increase in creativity have left the dieter's staple of yore — a canned peach half topped with a scoop of cottage cheese and served on a bed of tasteless limp lettuce — happily outmoded. New marriages of fruit and meat, seafood and vegetables have taken place. In this book, for example, chicken is coupled with grapefruit *(page 119)*, pork with nectarines and oranges *(page 122)*, prawns with pineapple and mangoes *(page 107)*, and kale with pears *(page 52)*, all to delicious effect.

Although the recipes call for fresh ingredients, salads of course can be a wonderful vehicle for leftovers. Providing they have not been previously buttered, cooked green beans, well chilled from their overnight stay in the refrigerator, make a lively luncheon dish when tossed with a vinaigrette. Likewise, leftover poultry and meats lend themselves to intriguing combinations with greens, fresh herbs and simple dressings.

Simplicity as a goal

With limitless possibilities for salads, the temptation has often been to put in too much. One·recipe from the 17th century calls for almonds, raisins, figs, spinach, olives, capers, currants, sage, cucumbers, red cabbage, orange and lemon. Our cooks have been more selective, balancing flavours and bearing in mind a particular salad's place in the meal as first course, main course or side dish. They have mixed complementary greens and paired foods and seasonings that share a natural affinity, such as tomatoes and basil, rice and saffron, cucumber and dill. At the same time, the cooks have sought contrasts in texture, combining, for instance, dried apricots, wild rice and water chestnuts *(page 70)*, or crab with spinach and sweetcorn *(page 110)*. They have also taken colour into account, and perhaps there are no more compelling examples than the oven-roasted vegetable salad with prawns and scallops on page 108, or the sweetcorn salad on page 17 with its strips of red and green peppers and bits of red onion.

The recipes have been designed to encourage imaginative, well-balanced eating. Serving portions are based on whether a salad is to be eaten as a side dish or a starter, as a main course at lunch, or as a main course at dinner. Salads with cooked ingredients are generally served in smaller portions because they are more substantial than raw salads. If you wish to serve larger portions, which means more calories, take into account the rest of the day's eating in your menu planning and compensate for the increased calories by selecting appropriate foods.

The first section of the book explores some unusual combinations of greens, vegetables and fruits. The second delves into grains, dried beans and pasta, while the third serves up salads based on meats, poultry and seafood. In the last section, the microwave oven offers shortcuts to salad-making. A gallery of the herbs used in the recipes appears on pages 138 and 139. Finally, there is a glossary on pages 140 and 141 which de-

scribes many of the ingredients and cooking terms in the book.

Whatever the components of a salad, it is the dressing that ties them together. In this book, each dressing has been created with an eye to limiting the fat and calories, generally through a reduction in the amount of oil used. Still, even reduced-oil dressings must contain calories. Thus anyone seriously concerned about lowering caloric intake should use a dressing sparingly, pouring on just enough to moisten and flavour the salad.

Handling salad ingredients

The success of a salad — particularly one calling for greens — depends greatly on how the ingredients are handled beforehand. If the salad is to be truly delicious, only the freshest of produce will do. Select greens that are crisp and well coloured. (The darker the lettuces, the more vitamin A they will contain.)

The greens should be washed under cold running water. With head lettuce, pluck away the leaves and pay particular attention to their bases, where soil may cling. Discard any leaves that are wilted, have frayed edges or are blemished. Grit-prone greens — spinach, for example — will come clean when gently swirled several times in a one or more bowls of water. Once they have been washed, the greens should be removed from the water, drained and then carefully dried — either by patting them between paper towels or by whirling them in a salad spinner. The removal of clinging water ensures that the dressing will coat the salad evenly and that the leaves will remain crisp.

If the washed greens are not to be used immediately, they may be stored for a day in the refrigerator, in a plastic bag, with a paper towel wrapped around them to soak up any excess moisture. Fresh herbs also benefit from respectful treatment; packed loosely in a closed container, they will remain vigorous a week or more in the refrigerator. Some cooks trim the stems, particularly of herbs that come in bunches, then stand the herbs in a glass or jar filled with water and keep them in the refrigerator lightly covered with plastic film.

For a natural-looking salad, tear the lettuce leaves by hand into pieces of the size you want — unless, of course, the recipe specifies otherwise. To preserve crispness, do this shortly before the salad is to be served and be sure to apply the dressing at the very last minute. Then toss or otherwise mix the salad.

Perhaps the wisest words about salad preparation are some that date back three centuries. "Every plant should bear its part without being overpowered by some herb of stronger taste, so as to endanger the native savour and virtue of the rest," wrote English diarist John Evelyn in 1699. When this is accomplished, all the ingredients should "fall into their places like notes in music". Thus carefully orchestrated, the salad will win applause as one of the liveliest, most satisfying and healthiest parts of the meal.

The Burgeoning of the Greens

Salad-making has benefited immeasurably from the increasing availability of hitherto esoteric or hard-to-find greens. Some of these are shown here and on the next three pages, with accompanying descriptions of their virtues. Among them are two vegetables, kale and beet greens, that take on new life when eaten raw in salads.

Curly endive. This resembles chicory in flavour. Although the lighter leaves are sweeter and more tender than the dark green ones, they still boast the tangy bite that is associated with all endives.

Beet greens. Use only the freshest, youngest greens, discarding the red stems. The leaves have a flavour that resembles both spinach and beetroot.

Rocket (arugula). An Italian green, rocket has a pungent, slightly peppery flavour. Look for small, narrow leaves — signs of a young, sweet plant.

Chicory. Sharp in flavour and crisp in texture, the finest chicory has tightly wrapped leaves that range in colour from white to pale yellow.

Dandelion greens. Part of the chicory family, dandelion greens should be eaten before the flower appears. Young leaves can be blanched by inverting a flowerpot over the plant.

Batavian endive (escarole). This broad-leaved relative of curly endive shares its cousin's pleasingly bitter flavour. It is best used in combination with sweeter greens.

Kale. A relative newcomer to the salad bowl, kale is an excellent source of vitamin C. Only the youngest leaves should be used, and many cooks prefer to shred them — they can be tough.

Lamb's lettuce (corn salad, mâche). Chewy but not crisp, this delicate green has a nutlike sweetness, with an underlying astringency. It complements dressings made with nut oils.

The Burgeoning of the Greens

Mustard greens (green-in-snow, Chinese mustard). With their pungent flavour, young mustard greens marry well with less assertive salad greens. Avoid the older, tougher leaves.

Chinese cabbage (Chinese leaves). This elongated cabbage has long, broad ribs and crinkled, white to light green leaves. Select unblemished heads with firm leaves.

Oakleaf lettuce. Among the most delicate of lettuces, oakleaf does not travel well. When available, however, it is well worth the purchase.

Savoy cabbage. The mildest form of head cabbage, Savoy can be used in salads where the taste of other cabbages would be too strong. Be sure the leaves are crisp.

Sorrel. A leaf vegetable resembling spinach, sorrel tastes of lemon. Use only the youngest leaves. When cooking sorrel, avoid reactive vessels and utensils; these can turn the sorrel black and give it a metallic taste.

Radicchio. This purplish red Italian chicory is sought for its chewy texture and slightly bitter taste. Italians call it "the flower that can be eaten".

Watercress. An aquatic green, watercress has a refreshing, peppery flavour. Buy bright green bunches with thin stems. Watercress can be refrigerated with its stems in water to keep it fresh.

The Key to Better Eating

Healthy Home Cooking addresses the concerns of today's weight-conscious, health-minded cooks with recipes that take into account guidelines set by nutritionists. The secret to eating well, of course, has to do with maintaining a balance of foods in the diet. The recipes thus should be used thoughtfully, in the context of a day's eating. To make the choice easier, this book presents an analysis of nutrients in a single serving of each salad recipe, as on the right. The counts for calories, protein, cholesterol, total fat, saturated fat and sodium are approximate. When the salad is to be served as a main course, the cook should seek to round out the meal's nutrition, supplying bread, for example, if the salad itself does not contain a starch.

Interpreting the chart

The chart below gives dietary guidelines for healthy men, women and children. Recommended figures vary from country to country, but the principles are the same everywhere. Here, the average daily amounts of calories and protein are from a report by the U.K. Department of Health and Social Security; the maximum advisable daily intake of fat is based on guidelines given by the National Advisory Committee on Nutrition Education (NACNE); those for cholesterol and sodium are based on upper limits suggested by the World Health Organization.

The volumes in the Healthy Home Cooking series do not purport to be diet books, nor do they focus on health foods. Rather, they express a commonsense approach to cooking that uses salt, sugar, cream, butter and oil in moderation while employing other ingredients that also provide flavour and satisfaction. Herbs, spices and aromatic vegetables, as well as fruits, peels, juices, wines and vinegars are all used towards this end.

In this volume, both safflower oil and virgin olive oil are favoured for salads. Safflower oil was chosen because it is the most highly polyunsaturated vegetable fat available in

Calories **104**
Protein **2g**
Cholesterol **0g**
Total fat **3g**
Saturated fat **0g**
Sodium **55mg**

supermarkets, and polyunsaturated fats reduce blood cholesterol; if unobtainable, use sunflower oil, also high in polyunsaturated fats. Virgin olive oil is used because it has a fine fruity flavour that is lacking in the lesser grade known as "pure". In addition, virgin olive oil is — like all olive oil — high in monounsaturated fats, which are thought not to increase blood cholesterol. Some cooks, seeking an even fruitier flavour, may wish to use extra virgin olive oil or even extra extra virgin, although the price will be higher, reflecting the quality of such an oil.

The recipes make few unusual demands. Naturally they call for fresh ingredients, offering substitutes when these are unavailable. (Only the original ingredient is calculated in the analysis, however.) Most of the ingredients can be found in any well-stocked supermarket. Any that may seem unusual are

described in a glossary on pages 140-141. In instances where particular techniques may be unfamiliar to a cook, there are appropriate how-to photographs.

In Healthy Home Cooking's test kitchens, heavy-bottomed pots and pans are used to guard against burning the food whenever a small amount of oil is used and where there is the possible danger of the food adhering to the hot surface, but non-stick pans can be utilized as well.

About cooking times

To help the cook plan ahead, Healthy Home Cooking takes time into account in its recipes. While recognizing that everyone cooks at a different speed, and that stoves and ovens differ, the series provides approximate "working" and "total" times for every dish. Working time stands for the minutes actively spent on preparation; total time includes unattended cooking time, as well as marinating or chilling. Since the recipes emphasize fresh foods, they may take a bit longer to prepare than dishes that call for canned or packaged products, but the payoff in flavour, and often in nutrition, should compensate for the little extra time involved.

Recommended Dietary Guidelines

		Average Daily Intake		Maximum Daily Intake			
		CALORIES	PROTEIN grams	CHOLESTEROL milligrams	TOTAL FAT grams	SATURATED FAT grams	SODIUM milligrams
Females	7-8	1900	47	300	80	32	2000*
	9-11	2050	51	300	77	35	2000
	12-17	2150	53	300	81	36	2000
	18-54	2150	54	300	81	36	2000
	54-74	1900	47	300	72	32	2000
Males	7-8	1980	49	300	80	33	2000
	9-11	2280	57	300	77	38	2000
	12-14	2640	66	300	99	44	2000
	15-17	2880	72	300	108	48	2000
	18-34	2900	72	300	109	48	2000
	35-64	2750	69	300	104	35	2000
	65-74	2400	60	300	91	40	2000

*(or 5g salt)

Basic Dressings with a New Twist

The low-fat, low-calorie dressings that follow were specially developed for this book. Several recipes call for them specifically, but the dressings can also be refrigerated for later use on salads of your own invention.

The vinaigrette suits fresh mixed greens of delicate flavour. The yogurt and buttermilk dressings marry well with assertive vegetables; they also complement meats, grains and pasta. The tofu-based mayonnaise makes an ideal partner for root vegetables as well as poultry and seafood and contains half the yolks and oil found in traditional versions.

Any of the four may be further enhanced by the addition of herbs, spices or other seasonings. The figures found beside each recipe give the nutrient analysis for one tablespoon of dressing.

New Mayonnaise

Makes 35 cl (12 fl oz)

125 g	firm tofu (bean curd), cut into small cubes and soaked in cold water for 10 minutes	4 oz
12.5 cl	plain low-fat yogurt, drained in a muslin-lined colander for 10 minutes	4 fl oz
1	egg yolk	1
1 tsp	dried mustard	1 tsp
12.5 cl	safflower oil	4 fl oz
4 tbsp	virgin olive oil	4 tbsp
2 tbsp	white wine vinegar or cider vinegar	2 tbsp
½ tsp	salt	½ tsp
½ tsp	sugar	½ tsp
⅛ tsp	white pepper	⅛ tsp

Calories **70**
Protein **1g**
Cholesterol **12mg**
Total fat **7g**
Saturated fat **1g**
Sodium **50mg**

Remove the tofu from its soaking water and drain it on paper towels. Transfer the tofu to a food processor or a blender. Add the yogurt, egg yolk and mustard, and process the mixture until it is very smooth, scraping down the sides at least once.

With the motor still running, pour in the oils in a thin, steady stream, stopping half way through the process to scrape the sides with a rubber spatula.

Add the vinegar, salt, sugar and pepper, and process the mayonnaise for 15 seconds more. Transfer the mayonnaise to a bowl and refrigerate it; the mayonnaise will keep for at least 10 days.

Vinaigrette

Makes about 12.5 cl (4 fl oz)

1 tsp	Dijon mustard	1 tsp
¼ tsp	salt	¼ tsp
	freshly ground black pepper	
2½ tbsp	red wine vinegar	2½ tbsp
2½ tbsp	safflower oil	2½ tbsp
2½ tbsp	virgin olive oil	2½ tbsp

Calories **75**
Protein **0g**
Cholesterol **0mg**
Total fat **8g**
Saturated fat **1g**
Sodium **75mg**

In a small bowl, combine the mustard, the salt, a grinding of pepper and the vinegar. Whisking vigorously, pour in the safflower oil in a thin, steady stream; incorporate the olive oil in the same way. Continue whisking until the dressing is well combined. Covered and stored in the refrigerator, the dressing will keep for about a week.

Buttermilk Dressing

Makes about 12.5 cl (4 fl oz)

12.5 cl	buttermilk	4 fl oz
	cayenne pepper	
¼ tsp	sugar	¼ tsp
1	shallot, finely chopped	1
4 tbsp	dried skimmed milk	4 tbsp
2 tbsp	fresh lemon juice	2 tbsp

Calories **15**
Protein **1g**
Cholesterol **1mg**
Total fat **0g**
Saturated fat **0g**
Sodium **30mg**

In a small bowl, combine the buttermilk, a pinch of cayenne pepper, the sugar and the shallot. Whisk in the dried milk a tablespoon at a time, then stir in the lemon juice. To allow the dressing to thicken, cover the bowl and refrigerate it for at least 30 minutes. The dressing will keep for three days.

EDITOR'S NOTE: *The inclusion of dried skimmed milk makes for a thick, creamy dressing.*

Creamy Yogurt Dressing

Makes about 12.5 cl (4 fl oz)

2 tbsp	cream sherry	2 tbsp
2	garlic cloves, finely chopped	2
1½ tsp	Dijon mustard	1½ tsp
12.5 cl	plain low-fat yogurt	4 fl oz
1 tbsp	soured cream	1 tbsp
⅛ tsp	white pepper	⅛ tsp

Calories **20**
Protein **1g**
Cholesterol **2mg**
Total fat **1g**
Saturated fat **0g**
Sodium **25mg**

Put the sherry and garlic into a small saucepan. Bring the mixture to a simmer over medium heat and cook it until nearly all the liquid has evaporated — about 3 minutes. Transfer the mixture to a bowl. Stir in the mustard, then the yogurt, soured cream and pepper. Cover the bowl and store the dressing in the refrigerator; it will keep for two to three days.

1 *High in fibre and nutrients, the offerings of garden and orchard afford the salad-maker ample room for delicious innovation.*

A Garden at the Table

Now that the opportunity for buying varied fresh ingredients has greatly increased, the cook can hardly fail to create a salad that is healthy, colourful and downright delicious every time. Still, most salad components benefit from careful handling if they are to keep all that is best about them. Certainly no one wants to sit down to a dish of limp lettuce, over-cooked vegetables or discoloured fruit, no matter how good the dressing.

In this section, salads made predominantly with vegetables or fruit, or combinations of both, are featured. Such vegetables as green beans, asparagus, cauliflower, broccoli, sliced carrots and courgettes are often steamed, blanched or parboiled to tenderize them. Cooked in this way (that is to say, briefly) they stay crunchy, and not only keep their colour — an essential feature in successful salad-making — but often become brighter. After being exposed to heat, the vegetables are then rinsed under cold running water to stop the cooking.

Since fruit is almost always eaten raw in a salad, it should be of juicy ripeness. Occasionally, though, a recipe will call for firm fruit; its texture and tartness can add real character to a dish. The mango and grape salad on page 60, for example, depends on the firmness of the mangoes for part of its effect.

Sliced into small pieces, with many exposed surfaces, both fruits and vegetables inevitably lose some of their nutrients. To minimize this loss, cut them up and add them to the salad as close to serving time as possible. Some fruit turns brown when it is exposed to air; use an old trick — rubbing the fruit with half a lemon or lime, or dribbling some of the juice over it — to prevent this. Not only will the fruit retain its colour, but the juice will supply a little extra vitamin C and a welcome bit of tartness.

Potato Salad with Peas and Sesame Seeds

Serves 8 as a side dish
Working time: about 25 minutes
Total time: about 1 hour and 15 minutes

Calories **140**
Protein **3g**
Cholesterol **0mg**
Total fat **6g**
Saturated fat **1g**
Sodium **70mg**

750 g	waxy potatoes	1½ lb
500 g	fresh peas, shelled, or 150 g (5 oz) frozen peas, thawed	1 lb
3 tbsp	sesame seeds	3 tbsp
½ tsp	cumin seeds	½ tsp
¼ tsp	cayenne pepper	¼ tsp
250 g	cucumber, peeled and coarsely chopped	8 oz
5	spring onions, trimmed and thinly sliced	5
3 tbsp	fresh lemon juice	3 tbsp
¼ tsp	salt	¼ tsp
2 tbsp	safflower oil	2 tbsp
¼ tsp	turmeric	¼ tsp
2	mildly hot green chili peppers, seeded, deribbed and quartered lengthwise (caution, box, opposite)	2

Boil the potatoes until they are soft when pierced with the tip of a sharp knife — about 25 minutes. Remove the potatoes from the water, halve them and set them aside to cool.

Meanwhile, parboil the fresh peas until they are tender — 4 to 5 minutes — or briefly blanch the frozen peas. Drain the peas and set them aside.

Heat a small, heavy frying pan over medium-high heat. When the pan is hot, add the sesame seeds, half of the cumin seeds and the cayenne pepper; toast the seeds, stirring constantly, until the sesame seeds turn light gold — about 1 minute. Transfer the mixture to a large bowl and let the seeds cool.

Peel the potatoes, then cut them into slices about 8 mm (⅓ inch) thick; halve the slices, and put them in the bowl with the sesame seed mixture. Grind the remaining cumin with a mortar and pestle and sprinkle it over the potatoes. Add the peas, cucumber, spring onions, lemon juice and salt to the bowl. Toss the ingredients well to combine them, and set aside.

Heat the safflower oil in a heavy frying pan over medium-high heat. When the oil is hot, reduce the heat to low and stir in the turmeric; immediately add the chili peppers and sauté them, stirring constantly, for 1 minute. Remove the chili pepper pieces and reserve them, and pour the contents of the pan over the potato mixture. Stir the salad gently to blend it, then transfer it to a serving platter. Garnish the salad with the reserved chilies. The salad may be served at room temperature or chilled.

Chili Peppers — a Cautionary Note

Both dried and fresh hot chili peppers should be handled with care. Their flesh and seeds contain volatile oils that can make skin tingle and cause eyes to burn. Rubber gloves offer protection — but the cook should still be careful not to touch the face, lips or eyes when working with chili peppers.

Soaking fresh chili peppers in cold, salted water for an hour will remove some of their fire. If canned chilies are substituted for fresh ones, they should be rinsed in cold water in order to eliminate as much of the brine used to preserve them as possible.

Sweet and Spicy Sweetcorn Salad

Serves 12 as a side dish
Working time: about 20 minutes
Total time: about 25 minutes

Calories **105**
Protein **2g**
Cholesterol **0mg**
Total fat **3g**
Saturated fat **0g**
Sodium **60mg**

825 g	fresh sweetcorn kernels (cut from about 5 large ears), or frozen sweetcorn kernels, thawed	1¾ lb
1	sweet red pepper, seeded, deribbed and cut into thin, 2.5 cm (1 inch) long strips	1
1	sweet green pepper, seeded, deribbed and cut into thin, 2.5 cm (1 inch) long strips	1
2	small hot green chili peppers, seeded, deribbed and finely chopped (caution, box, above)	2
1	small red onion, chopped	1
4 tbsp	red wine vinegar	4 tbsp
1 tbsp	brown sugar	1 tbsp
2 tbsp	safflower oil	2 tbsp
2 tsp	chopped fresh oregano, or ½ tsp dried oregano	2 tsp
¼ tsp	salt	¼ tsp
	freshly ground black pepper	

Pour enough water into a saucepan to fill it about 2.5 cm (1 inch) deep. Set a vegetable steamer in the pan and bring the water to the boil. Put the fresh sweetcorn into the steamer, cover the pan, and steam the sweetcorn until it is just tender — about 3 minutes. (Frozen sweetcorn does not require steaming.)

In a large bowl, combine the wine vinegar, sugar, oil, oregano, salt and pepper. Add the sweetcorn, the peppers and the onion, and toss the mixture well. Serve the salad at room temperature, or refrigerate it for at least 1 hour and serve it well chilled.

Greens with Violets and Wild Strawberries

VIOLET BLOSSOMS, WHEN AVAILABLE, ADD A DELICIOUS DELICACY TO A SIMPLE GREEN SALAD. PICK THE BLOSSOMS JUST BEFORE SERVING TIME. DO NOT USE VIOLETS FROM A FLORIST — THEY MAY HAVE BEEN SPRAYED WITH CHEMICALS.

Serves 4 as a first course or side dish
Working time: about 10 minutes
Total time: about 15 minutes

Calories **60**
Protein **1g**
Cholesterol **0mg**
Total fat **5g**
Saturated fat **1g**
Sodium **25mg**

1 tbsp	raspberry vinegar	1 tbsp
1 tbsp	finely chopped shallot	1 tbsp
½ tsp	Dijon mustard	½ tsp
	freshly ground black pepper	
1½ tbsp	unsalted chicken stock	1½ tbsp
1½ tbsp	virgin olive oil	1½ tbsp
250 g	mixed salad greens, washed and dried	8 oz
4 tbsp	sweet violet blossoms (optional)	4 tbsp
4 tbsp	wild strawberries (optional)	4 tbsp

Combine the vinegar, shallot, mustard and some pepper in a small bowl. Let the mixture stand for 5 minutes; whisk in the stock, then the oil. Toss the greens with the dressing. Strew the violets and the strawberries, if using, over the top; serve immediately.

EDITOR'S NOTE: *The greens here include Batavian endive, chicory, watercress and red oakleaf lettuce; any similar combination of mild and bitter greens would be appropriate.*

Red Cabbage Salad with Spiced Vinegar Dressing

Serves 6 as a side dish
Working time: about 15 minutes
Total time: about 1 hour and 15 minutes

Calories **100**
Protein **3g**
Cholesterol **0mg**
Total fat **8g**
Saturated fat **2g**
Sodium **170mg**

350 g	red cabbage, finely shredded	12 oz
½ tsp	salt	½ tsp
4 tbsp	red wine vinegar	4 tbsp
1	blade of mace	1
1	bay leaf	1
8	peppercorns	8
½ tsp	mustard seeds	½ tsp
4	allspice	4
2	dried red chili peppers	2
1	small sweet green pepper, seeded, deribbed and finely sliced	1
1	small onion, halved and finely sliced	1
3	sticks celery, finely sliced	3
30 g	pine-nuts, lightly toasted	1 oz
2 tbsp	virgin olive oil	2 tbsp
1	garlic clove, crushed	1
¼ tsp	sugar	¼ tsp
	freshly ground black pepper	

Put the shredded cabbage into a large salad bowl, sprinkle with the salt and toss lightly together. Cover the bowl and set it aside in a cool place for 1 hour.

Meanwhile, put the vinegar into a small saucepan with the mace, bay leaf, peppercorns, allspice and chili peppers. Bring to the boil, then boil gently until the vinegar is reduced to 1 tablespoonful. Allow to cool. Add the sliced green pepper, onion, celery and toasted pine-nuts to the red cabbage.

Strain the cold vinegar into a small bowl and add the oil, garlic, sugar and freshly ground pepper to taste. Whisk lightly together. Pour this dressing over the red cabbage and toss well. Serve at once.

Wrapped Salads

THIS RECIPE CALLS FOR CUTTING THE VEGETABLES INTO BÂTONNETS, FRENCH FOR "LITTLE STICKS". BÂTONNETS ARE ABOUT 4 CM (1½ INCHES) LONG AND 5 MM (¼ INCH) SQUARE.

Serves 6 as a first course
Working time: about 1 hour
Total time: about 1 hour and 45 minutes

Calories **85**
Protein **2g**
Cholesterol **0mg**
Total fat **4g**
Saturated fat **0g**
Sodium **220mg**

2	fennel bulbs, green tops removed, bulbs cut into bâtonnets	2
250 g	turnips, peeled and cut into bâtonnets	8 oz
500 g	courgettes, cut into bâtonnets	1 lb
2	oranges, juice of 1, pared rind of both	2
6	large Savoy cabbage leaves	6
1	small red onion, finely chopped	1
1½ tbsp	safflower oil	1½ tbsp
2 tbsp	finely chopped fresh chervil or parsley	2 tbsp
½ tsp	salt	½ tsp
	freshly ground black pepper	
6	sprigs fresh chervil or parsley for garnish	6

Bring 2 litres (3½ pints) of water to the boil in a large pan. Place the fennel bâtonnets in a sieve; lower the sieve part way into the boiling water and blanch the bâtonnets until they are tender but still slightly crunchy — 2 to 3 minutes. Refresh the fennel under cold running water, drain it well, and transfer it to a large bowl. Blanch the turnip bâtonnets the same way for 2 to 3 minutes; refresh them and transfer them to the bowl. Blanch the courgette pieces for about 1 minute; refresh them, too, and put them in the bowl.

Use the sieve to blanch the orange rind in the boiling water for 10 seconds; refresh the rind under cold running water and drain it well. Finely chop the rind and transfer it to the bowl with the bâtonnets.

Boil the cabbage leaves in the same pan of water until they are pliable but not too soft — about 15 ▶

seconds. Drain the leaves; when they are cool enough to handle, use a V-shaped cut to remove the thick core from the stem end of each leaf. Set the leaves aside.

Add the onion, oil, orange juice, chopped chervil or parsley, salt and some pepper to the bowl with the bâtonnets; toss the mixture well, then refrigerate the salad for about 15 minutes.

Spread the cabbage leaves out on a work surface. Using a slotted spoon, divide the salad evenly among the leaves. Gather the edges of a leaf over its filling; gently twist the edges closed, forming a pouch. Repeat the process to enclose the other five mounds of filling.

Place the cabbage bundles in a shallow dish and pour the dressing remaining in the bowl over the top and sides of each one. Chill the salads for about 30 minutes before serving them, garnished with the chervil or parsley sprigs.

Carrot, Swede and Watercress Salad

Serves 6 as a side dish
Working (and total) time: about 40 minutes

Calories **60**
Protein **1g**
Cholesterol **0mg**
Total fat **3g**
Saturated fat **0g**
Sodium **70mg**

4 tsp	virgin olive oil	4 tsp
3	carrots, halved lengthwise, the halves cut diagonally into 5 mm (¼ inch) slices	3
325 g	swedes, peeled and cut into bâtonnets	11 oz
1	shallot, halved, the halves quartered	1
⅛ tsp	salt	⅛ tsp
¼ tsp	cayenne pepper	¼ tsp
	freshly ground black pepper	
4 tbsp	cider vinegar	4 tbsp
1	bunch of watercress, stemmed, washed and dried	1

Heat the oil in a large, heavy frying pan over medium heat. When the oil is hot, add the carrots, swedes,

shallot, salt, cayenne pepper and some black pepper. Cook the mixture, stirring frequently, until the vegetables are tender but still crisp — about 7 minutes. Pour the vinegar into the pan and continue cooking, stirring frequently, until almost all of the vinegar has evaporated — 1 to 2 minutes. Stir in the watercress and cook it until it has just wilted — about 30 seconds. Transfer the salad to a serving plate and let it cool just slightly before serving it.

Cucumber and Citrus Salad

Serves 4 as a side dish
Working (and total) time: about 25 minutes

Calories **80**
Protein **2g**
Cholesterol **0mg**
Total fat **1g**
Saturated fat **0g**
Sodium **135mg**

1	large cucumber, cut into 5 cm (2 inch) long segments	1
1 tsp	virgin olive oil	1 tsp
1 tsp	chopped fresh rosemary, or ¼ tsp crushed dried rosemary	1 tsp
	freshly ground black pepper	
1	pink grapefruit	1
2	large juicy oranges	2
2 tbsp	fresh lime juice	2 tbsp
4 tbsp	fresh orange juice	4 tbsp
4 tbsp	fresh grapefruit juice	4 tbsp
1 tsp	red wine vinegar	1 tsp
¼ tsp	salt	¼ tsp
1	spring onion, cut into 5 cm (2 inch) long julienne	1

Using an apple corer, a melon baller or a small spoon, remove the core of seeds from each cucumber segment. Slice the segments into rings about 3 mm (⅛ inch) thick. Toss the rings with the oil, rosemary and a generous grinding of pepper.

Working over a bowl to catch the juice, cut away the peel, white pith and outer membrane from the grape-

fruit and oranges. To separate the segments from the inner membranes, slice down to the core with a sharp knife on either side of each segment; set the segments aside. Cut each grapefuit segment in half; leave the orange segments whole. Set the bowl containing the juice aside.

Arrange the cucumber slices in a large, deep plate and position the citrus segments on top. If you are preparing the salad in advance, it may be refrigerated for up to 2 hours at this point.

Combine the lime juice, orange juice, grapefruit juice, vinegar and salt with the reserved juice in the bowl. Pour this dressing over the salad; scatter the spring onion over the top just before serving.

Asparagus and Jerusalem Artichoke Salad

Serves 4 as a first course
Working (and total) time: about 20 minutes

Calories **45**
Protein **2g**
Cholesterol **0mg**
Total fat **1g**
Saturated fat **0g**
Sodium **5mg**

1	lemon, cut in half	1
125 g	Jerusalem artichokes, scrubbed well	4 oz
500 g	asparagus, trimmed, peeled and cut diagonally into 4 cm (1 ½ inch) lengths	1 lb
1 tsp	walnut oil or virgin olive oil	1 tsp
1 tbsp	cut fresh dill	1 tbsp

Make acidulated water by squeezing the juice of a lemon half into a small bowl of cold water. Peel and slice the Jerusalem artichokes, dropping them into the water as you work.

Pour enough water into a saucepan to fill it about 2.5 cm (1 inch) deep. Set a vegetable steamer in the pan and bring the water to the boil. Put the artichoke slices into the steamer, cover the pan tightly, and steam the slices until they are tender when pierced with a knife — about 5 minutes. Transfer the slices to a bowl and toss them with the juice of the other lemon half.

While the artichokes are steaming, cook the asparagus. Pour enough water into a large sauté pan to fill it about 2.5 cm (1 inch) deep. Bring the water to the boil, add the asparagus pieces, and cook them until they are tender — about 4 minutes. Drain the asparagus and refresh the pieces under cold water. Drain the pieces once again and toss them with the oil.

Arrange the asparagus on a large serving platter or on four small plates. Top the asparagus with the artichoke slices; sprinkle the dill over all before serving.

Julienned Carrots, Mange-Tout and Chicory

Serves 6 as a first course or side dish
Working (and total) time: about 20 minutes

Calories **60**
Protein **2g**
Cholesterol **0mg**
Total fat **4g**
Saturated fat **0g**
Sodium **70mg**

1 tbsp	very finely chopped shallot	1 tbsp
1	garlic clove, lightly crushed	1
1 tbsp	herb vinegar or white wine vinegar	1 tbsp
1½ tbsp	almond oil or walnut oil	1½ tbsp
⅛ tsp	salt	⅛ tsp
	freshly ground black pepper	
75 g	carrots, julienned	2½ oz
150 g	mange-tout, julienned	5 oz
250 g	chicory, cored and julienned	8 oz

In a large bowl, combine the shallot, garlic and vinegar. Whisk in the oil and season the dressing with the salt and some pepper. Set the dressing aside while you prepare the vegetables.

Add the carrot julienne to 1 litre (1¾ pints) of boiling water and cook it for 1 minute. Add the mange-tout and cook the vegetables for only 15 seconds longer. Briefly refresh the vegetables under cold running water, then drain them well. Remove the garlic from the dressing and discard it. Add the cooked vegetables and the chicory to the dressing. Toss the salad well and serve it immediately.

Six-Treasure Asian Medley

Serves 10 as a side dish
Working (and total) time: about 40 minutes

Calories **70**
Protein **2g**
Cholesterol **0mg**
Total fat **4g**
Saturated fat **0g**
Sodium **220mg**

350 g	carrots	12 oz
125 g	mange-tout, strings removed	4 oz
350 g	small cucumbers	12 oz
4 tbsp	sliced water chestnuts	4 tbsp
250 g	Chinese cabbage, sliced crosswise into 1 cm (½ inch) thick strips	8 oz
1	sweet red pepper, seeded, deribbed and julienned	1
Ginger-sesame dressing		
1 tsp	Sichuan peppercorns	1 tsp
1 tsp	dry mustard	1 tsp
2 tsp	sugar	2 tsp
3 tbsp	rice vinegar	3 tbsp
3 tbsp	low-sodium soy sauce or shoyu	3 tbsp
2 tsp	dark sesame oil	2 tsp
2 tbsp	safflower oil	2 tbsp
1 tbsp	finely chopped fresh ginger root	1 tbsp
3	garlic cloves, finely chopped	3

With a small paring knife or a cannelle knife, cut a shallow groove running the length of each carrot. Repeat the cut on the opposite side of each carrot, then slice the carrots diagonally into ovals about 3 mm (⅛ inch) thick. Put the pieces in a saucepan and pour in enough cold water to cover them by about 5 cm (2 inches). Bring the water to the boil. Reduce the heat and simmer the carrots until they are barely tender — about 2 minutes. Drain the carrots and transfer them to a large bowl.

Cut a V-shaped notch in each end of each mange-tout. Blanch them in boiling water for 30 seconds. Refresh the mange-tout under cold running water, drain them well, and add them to the bowl with the carrots.

Peel the cucumbers, leaving four narrow strips of skin attached to each one. Halve the cucumbers lengthwise; scoop out the seeds with a melon baller or a teaspoon. Cut the cucumber halves into 3 mm (⅛ inch) thick slices. Add the cucumber slices, water chestnuts, cabbage and red pepper to the bowl containing the carrots and mange-tout.

To prepare the dressing, put the Sichuan peppercorns into a small frying pan and set it over medium-high heat. Cook the peppercorns until you see the first wisps of smoke. Transfer the peppercorns to a mortar or a small bowl and crush them with a pestle or the heel of a heavy knife. Whisk together the mustard, sugar, vinegar, soy sauce, sesame oil, safflower oil, peppercorns, ginger and garlic. Toss the vegetables with the dressing and serve at once.

Charcoal-Grilled Summer Salad

Serves 8 as a side dish
Working time: about 1 hour
Total time: about 1 hour and 30 minutes

Calories **95**
Protein **3g**
Cholesterol **0mg**
Total fat **5g**
Saturated fat **1g**
Sodium **115mg**

1	large aubergine	1
½ tsp	salt	½ tsp
2	large courgettes	2
½ tsp	virgin olive oil	½ tsp
	freshly ground black pepper	
2	sweet red peppers	2
250 g	Batavian endive or rocket, stemmed, washed and dried	8 oz
4	ripe tomatoes, halved lengthwise	4
1	small red onion, very thinly sliced	1

Garlic and herb dressing		
1	whole garlic bulb, the papery top cut off to expose the cloves	1
5 tsp	virgin olive oil	5 tsp
1 tbsp	fresh lemon juice	1 tbsp
1 tbsp	chopped fresh parsley	1 tbsp
½ tbsp	fresh thyme, or ½ tsp dried thyme	½ tbsp
½ tbsp	chopped fresh oregano, or ½ tsp dried oregano	½ tbsp
⅛ tsp	salt	⅛ tsp
	freshly ground black pepper	
1 tbsp	walnut or safflower oil	1 tbsp

To begin the dressing, first preheat the oven to 180°C (350°F or Mark 4). Place the garlic bulb on a piece of aluminium foil and dribble ½ teaspoon of the olive oil over the exposed cloves. Fold the foil tightly around the bulb and roast the garlic until it is very soft — about

1 hour. Approximately half way through the roasting time, light the charcoal in an outdoor barbecue. When the garlic bulb is cool enough to handle, remove the cloves from their skins and set them aside.

While the garlic is roasting, peel the aubergine and cut it lengthwise into eight slices. Sprinkle the ½ teaspoon of salt over the slices and let them stand for at least 30 minutes to neutralize their natural bitterness. Rinse the slices to rid them of the salt, and pat them dry with paper towels. Cut each of the courgettes lengthwise into four slices. Brush the aubergine and courgette slices with the ½ teaspoon of olive oil. Sprinkle the vegetables with some pepper and set them aside.

When the charcoal is hot, place the red peppers on the rack; turn them as they scorch, until their skins are blistered on all sides — 10 to 15 minutes. Transfer the peppers to a bowl and cover it with plastic film; the trapped steam will loosen the skins.

Grill the aubergine and courgette slices until they are golden-brown but retain their shape — about 5 minutes per side. Remove the vegetables from the barbecue and let them cool to room temperature.

With a paring knife, peel the peppers. Seed and derib them, then quarter them lengthwise. Set the pepper pieces aside.

To finish the dressing, press the reserved garlic cloves through a sieve into a small bowl. Add the lemon juice, parsley, thyme, oregano, ⅛ teaspoon of salt and some pepper; stir well to combine the ingredients. Whisking vigorously, pour in the remaining olive oil in a thin, steady stream; incorporate the walnut or safflower oil the same way, and continue whisking until the dressing is thoroughly combined.

Arrange the endive or rocket on a large platter to form a bed for the other vegetables. Position the aubergine, courgettes, red peppers, tomatoes and onion in rows on the greens. Pour the dressing over the vegetables and serve.

Shiitake Mushroom Salad

Serves 4 as a first course
Working time: about 20 minutes
Total time: about 30 minutes

Calories **95**
Protein **2g**
Cholesterol **0mg**
Total fat **5g**
Saturated fat **1g**
Sodium **150mg**

1½ tbsp	virgin olive oil	1½ tbsp
50 g	thinly sliced shallots	1½ oz
250 g	fresh shiitake mushrooms or field mushrooms, stemmed and wiped clean, caps sliced	8 oz
2 tsp	fresh thyme, or ½ tsp dried thyme	2 tsp
¼ tsp	salt	¼ tsp
2	ripe tomatoes, seeded and cut into 5 mm (¼ inch) wide strips	2
2 tbsp	balsamic vinegar, or 1½ tbsp red wine vinegar mixed with ½ tsp honey	2 tbsp
1 tbsp	fresh lemon juice	1 tbsp
	freshly ground black pepper	
1 tbsp	chopped fresh parsley	1 tbsp
4	large Chinese cabbage leaves or cos lettuce leaves for garnish	4

Heat the olive oil in a large, heavy frying pan over medium heat. Add the shallots, mushrooms and thyme, and cook them, stirring frequently, for 7 minutes. Sprinkle with the salt, then stir in the tomatoes, vinegar, lemon juice and some pepper. Cook, stirring often, until the tomatoes are soft — about 4 minutes. Stir in the parsley and remove the pan from the heat. Let the mixture stand until it is tepid.

Place a cabbage or lettuce leaf on each of four plates; divide the salad evenly among the leaves.

Bean Sprouts in a Sesame Vinaigrette

Serves 8 as a side dish
Working time: about 10 minutes
Total time: about 25 minutes

Calories **50**
Protein **2g**
Cholesterol **0mg**
Total fat **3g**
Saturated fat **0g**
Sodium **80mg**

2 tbsp	Chinese black vinegar or balsamic vinegar	2 tbsp
1 tbsp	low-sodium soy sauce or shoyu	1 tbsp
1 tbsp	safflower oil	1 tbsp
1 tsp	dark sesame oil	1 tsp
1½ tsp	sugar	1½ tsp
500 g	fresh mung bean sprouts (page 37)	1 lb
1 tbsp	sesame seeds	1 tbsp
1	spring onion, trimmed, finely chopped	1

Bring 3 litres (5 pints) of water to the boil in a large pan. While the water is heating, combine the vinegar, soy sauce, safflower oil, sesame oil and sugar in a small bowl.

Immerse the bean sprouts in the boiling water; stir them once and drain them immediately. Refresh the sprouts under cold running water, then transfer them to a bowl lined with a clean cloth; the cloth will absorb the water. Refrigerate for at least 10 minutes.

Remove the cloth, leaving the sprouts in the bowl. Pour the dressing over the sprouts and toss the salad well. Chill the salad for 5 minutes more and toss it once again. Sprinkle the sesame seeds and chopped spring onion over the top, and serve at once.

Asian-Style Cucumber Salad

Serves 6 as a side dish
Working time: about 30 minutes
Total time: about 3 hours (includes chilling)

Calories **35**
Protein **0g**
Cholesterol **0mg**
Total fat **3g**
Saturated fat **0g**
Sodium **5mg**

2 tbsp	rice vinegar	2 tbsp
1	garlic clove, finely chopped	1
1 tsp	finely chopped fresh ginger root	1 tsp
1 tsp	mirin (sweet Japanese rice wine)	1 tsp
¼ tsp	dark sesame oil	¼ tsp
1 tbsp	peanut or safflower oil	1 tbsp
1	large cucumber	1
30 g	carrot, julienned	1 oz
30 g	yellow squash or courgette, julienned	1 oz
4 tbsp	radish sprouts (optional; page 37)	4 tbsp

Combine the vinegar, garlic, ginger, mirin, sesame oil, and peanut or safflower oil in a bowl. Set the vinaigrette aside.

With a cannelle knife or a paring knife, cut four shallow lengthwise grooves in the cucumber. Halve the cucumber lengthwise. Thinly slice the cucumber halves.

Put the cucumber, carrot, squash or courgette, and radish sprouts in the vinaigrette; stir well. Refrigerate the mixture for 2 to 3 hours before serving.

A Potpourri of Vegetables Bathed in Balsamic Vinegar

Serves 8 as a first course
Working time: about 40 minutes
Total time: about 50 minutes

Calories **80**
Protein **3g**
Cholesterol **0mg**
Total fat **4g**
Saturated fat **1g**
Sodium **135mg**

2½ tbsp	virgin olive oil	2½ tbsp
3	shallots, thinly sliced	3
1	garlic clove, finely chopped	1
1	bunch beet greens with stems, washed and thinly sliced (about 125 g/4 oz)	1
¼ tsp	salt	¼ tsp
	freshly ground black pepper	
6 tbsp	balsamic vinegar	6 tbsp
2	carrots, halved lengthwise and sliced diagonally into 1 cm (½ inch) pieces	2
2	small turnips, peeled and cut into bâtonnets	2
150 g	small broccoli florets	5 oz
250 g	courgettes, halved lengthwise and sliced diagonally into 1 cm (½ inch) pieces	8 oz
125 g	small yellow squash or courgettes, halved lengthwise and sliced diagonally into 1 cm (½ inch) pieces	4 oz

Pour 3 litres (5 pints) of water into a large pan; add 1 teaspoon of salt and bring the water to the boil.

In the meantime, heat 1½ tablespoons of the oil in a large, heavy frying pan set over medium heat. Add the shallots and garlic, and cook them for 2 minutes. Stir in the beet greens and their stems, the ¼ teaspoon of salt and some pepper. Cook the mixture, stirring frequently, for 7 minutes. Pour the vinegar over the mixture, stir well, and remove the pan from the heat.

Put the carrots into the boiling water and cook them for 1 minute. Add the turnips and broccoli to the carrots in the pan, and cook them for 2 minutes. Add the courgettes and yellow squash to the pan, and cook all the vegetables together for only 30 seconds more. Immediately drain the vegetables and refresh them under cold running water; when they are cool, drain them on paper towels.

Transfer the vegetables to a bowl and pour the contents of the frying pan over them. Dribble the remaining tablespoon of oil over the top, add a liberal grinding of pepper, and toss the salad well. Chill the salad for at least 10 minutes. Toss it once more before presenting it at the table.

EDITOR'S NOTE: *If beet greens are not available, Swiss chard leaves can be substituted.*

Alfalfa Sprouts and Red Onion Salad

Serves 4 as a first course
Working (and total) time: about 15 minutes

Calories **75**
Protein **1g**
Cholesterol **0mg**
Total fat **5g**
Saturated fat **0g**
Sodium **70mg**

1	large juicy orange	1
1 tbsp	fresh lemon juice	1 tbsp
1 tbsp	safflower oil	1 tbsp
1 tsp	virgin olive oil	1 tsp
1 tsp	fresh thyme, or ¼ tsp dried thyme	1 tsp
½ tsp	sugar	½ tsp
⅛ tsp	salt	⅛ tsp
	freshly ground black pepper	
1	red onion, sliced into paper-thin rounds, the rings separated	1
45 g	alfalfa sprouts (page 37)	1½ oz

Working over a bowl to catch the juice, cut away the peel, white pith and outer membrane from the orange. To separate the segments from the inner membranes, slice down to the core with a sharp knife on either side of each segment and set the segments aside. Squeeze the remaining membranes over the bowl to extract any juice.

Stir the lemon juice, safflower oil, olive oil, thyme, sugar, salt and some pepper into the juice in the bowl. Whisk the dressing well.

Put the onion rings into a bowl and pour half of the dressing over them. Add a generous grinding of pepper and toss well. In the other bowl, combine the alfalfa sprouts with the remaining dressing.

Spread equal amounts of the onion rings on four plates. Mound one quarter of the sprouts in the centre of each bed of onions, then garnish each serving with the orange segments. Serve immediately.

Tomato Fans with Basil, Prosciutto and Provolone

Serves 4 as a first course or side dish
Working time: about 20 minutes
Total time: about 35 minutes

Calories **105**
Protein **5g**
Cholesterol **11mg**
Total fat **7g**
Saturated fat **2g**
Sodium **280mg**

2	large ripe tomatoes, cored	2
¼ tsp	sugar	¼ tsp
⅛ tsp	salt	⅛ tsp
	freshly ground black pepper	
2 tbsp	red wine vinegar	2 tbsp
1	shallot, finely chopped	1
1 tbsp	virgin olive oil	1 tbsp
2	garlic cloves, crushed	2
45 g	thinly sliced prosciutto, julienned	1½ oz
30 g	provolone cheese, thinly sliced and julienned	1 oz
2 tbsp	thinly sliced fresh basil leaves	2 tbsp
1	round lettuce (about 125 g/4 oz), washed and dried	1

Halve the tomatoes from top to bottom, then, with the cut side down, thinly slice each half, and set it aside intact. Transfer the sliced halves to a plate. Gently fan out each half. Sprinkle the tomatoes with the sugar, salt and a generous grinding of black pepper, then dribble 1 tablespoon of the wine vinegar over them. Refrigerate the tomato fans for about 10 minutes.

Meanwhile, prepare the dressing. Put the finely chopped shallot and the remaining tablespoon of vinegar into a bowl. Whisk in the oil. Add the garlic, prosciutto, provolone cheese, basil and some more pepper, and stir the mixture to combine it; set it aside.

Arrange the lettuce on a serving platter and place the tomato fans on the leaves. Remove the garlic cloves from the dressing and spoon a quarter of it on each tomato fan. Serve the salad immediately.

Baby Leeks in Caper-Cream Vinaigrette

Serves 6 as a first course
Working time: about 20 minutes
Total time: about 45 minutes

Calories **190**
Protein **2g**
Cholesterol **3mg**
Total fat **4g**
Saturated fat **1g**
Sodium **200mg**

12	baby leeks (about 750 g/1½ lb), trimmed, green tops cut to within 5 cm (2 inches) of the white part	12
2 tsp	fresh thyme, or ½ tsp dried thyme	2 tsp
2	shallots, finely chopped	2
¼ tsp	salt	¼ tsp
	freshly ground black pepper	
1 tbsp	fresh lemon juice	1 tbsp
1 tbsp	red wine vinegar	1 tbsp
1 tsp	capers, rinsed and chopped	1 tsp
1 tbsp	virgin olive oil	1 tbsp
2 tbsp	single cream	2 tbsp
2 tbsp	chopped sweet red pepper	2 tbsp
1	garlic clove, very finely chopped	1

Wash each leek to remove the grit: without splitting the leek or detaching any leaves, gently prise apart the leaves and run cold water between them to force out the dirt. Shake the excess water from the leaves and repeat the washing process. Arrange the leeks in a pan large enough to hold them in a single layer. Pour in just enough water to cover the leeks; add the thyme, half of the shallots, ⅛ teaspoon of the salt and a lavish grinding of pepper. Poach the leeks over medium-low heat for 10 minutes. Gently turn the leeks over, and continue poaching them until they are tender —about 10 minutes more. Transfer the leeks to a plate lined with a double thickness of paper towels. Refrigerate the leeks until they are cool — at least 20 minutes.

About 10 minutes before the leeks are sufficiently chilled, combine the remaining shallots in a small bowl with the lemon juice, vinegar, capers, the remaining ⅛ teaspoon of salt and some more pepper. Let the vinaigrette stand for 5 minutes, then whisk in the oil, cream, red pepper and garlic.

Transfer the cooled leeks to a serving dish. Pour the vinaigrette over the leeks and serve them at once.

Curried Cabbage Coleslaw

Serves 6 as a side dish
Working time: about 20 minutes
Total time: about 1 hour and 20 minutes

Calories **60**
Protein **2g**
Cholesterol **4mg**
Total fat **2g**
Saturated fat **1g**
Sodium **145mg**

15 cl	soured cream	5 fl oz
2 tsp	curry powder	2 tsp
2 tsp	tomato paste	2 tsp
2 tsp	lemon juice	2 tsp
½ tsp	salt	½ tsp
	freshly ground black pepper	
500 g	white cabbage, finely shredded	1 lb
1	red apple, quartered, cored and thinly sliced	1
40 g	raisins	1½ oz
1 tbsp	chopped fresh coriander	1 tbsp

Put the soured cream, curry powder, tomato paste, lemon juice, salt and some freshly ground pepper into a large bowl and stir well. Add the shredded cabbage, sliced apple and the raisins and mix well together. Cover the bowl, then set it aside in a cool place for at least 1 hour to allow the flavours to mellow.

Just before serving, spoon the salad into a serving bowl and garnish with the coriander.

Dandelion Greens with Potato and Bacon

THE PLEASINGLY PUNGENT LEAVES OF THE DANDELION MAKE FOR A BRACING SALAD. HARVEST THE BRIGHT GREEN LEAVES IN THE SPRING; THE DARKER LEAVES THAT GROW IN THE SUMMER HAVE A BITTER TASTE.

Serves 4 as a first course
Working time: about 30 minutes
Total time: about 45 minutes

Calories **130**
Protein **5g**
Cholesterol **9mg**
Total fat **6g**
Saturated fat **1g**
Sodium **265mg**

1	large waxy potato	1
1 tbsp	safflower oil	1 tbsp
45 g	mild back bacon, julienned	1½ oz
2	shallots, thinly sliced	2
2 tbsp	red wine vinegar	2 tbsp
4 tbsp	unsalted chicken stock	4 tbsp
½ tsp	sugar	½ tsp
⅛ tsp	salt	⅛ tsp
	freshly ground black pepper	
250 g	dandelion greens, washed and dried	8 oz

Boil the potato until it is barely tender — about 15 minutes. Remove the potato from the water and set it aside until it is cool enough to handle. Peel the potato and cut it into small dice.

Heat the safflower oil in a heavy frying pan over medium-high heat. Add the bacon and shallots, and sauté them until the bacon begins to brown — 4 to 5 minutes. Add the diced potato and continue sautéing until the potato pieces begin to brown too — about 3 minutes more.

Stir in the vinegar and cook the mixture for 2 minutes. Add the stock, sugar, salt and some pepper; cook the mixture, stirring often, until the liquid is reduced by half — about 3 minutes.

Pour the contents of the pan over the dandelion greens and toss well; serve the salad immediately.

Moulded Leek Salads

Serves 4 as a first course
Working time: about 30 minutes
Total time: about 2 hours and 30 minutes

Calories **80**	350 g	leeks, trimmed, split, washed thoroughly to remove all grit, and sliced crosswise into 5 mm (¼ inch) thick pieces	12 oz
Protein **6g**			
Cholesterol **2mg**			
Total fat **1g**	¼ litre	cold unsalted chicken stock	8 fl oz
Saturated fat **0g**	1 tbsp	fresh lemon juice	1 tbsp
Sodium **80mg**	1 tbsp	powdered gelatine	1 tbsp
	12.5 cl	plain low-fat yogurt	4 fl oz
	½ tbsp	Dijon mustard	½ tbsp
	4 tbsp	finely chopped parsley	4 tbsp
	1 tbsp	finely cut fresh chives	1 tbsp
		freshly ground black pepper	
		watercress sprigs for garnish	

Add the leeks to 2 litres (3½ pints) of water boiling in a pan. Return the water to the boil and cook the leeks until they are tender — about 2 minutes. Drain the leeks thoroughly and allow them to cool.

In a bowl, combine half of the stock with the lemon juice. Sprinkle the gelatine on top of the liquid and allow it to soften. Meanwhile, heat the remaining stock in a small saucepan over low heat. Pour the gelatine mixture into the pan, then stir gently until the gelatine dissolves. Return the gelatine mixture to the bowl and set the bowl in a larger vessel filled with ice cubes. Whisk in the yogurt and mustard. Chill the mixture, stirring it from time to time. When it begins to set — after about 20 minutes — fold in the leeks, parsley, chives and some pepper.

Rinse four 12.5 cl (4 fl oz) ramekins with cold water. Shake the ramekins dry, leaving a few drops of water clinging inside. Divide the leek mixture evenly among the ramekins, then chill them until the mixture is firm — about 2 hours.

To serve the moulded salads, run the tip of a knife around the inside of each ramekin. Dip the bottoms of the ramekins in hot water for about 15 seconds, then unmould the salads on to individual plates. Garnish each one with a few sprigs of watercress and serve at once.

Batavian Endive Chiffonade with Peppers

Serves 6 as a side dish
Working time: about 20 minutes
Total time: about 45 minutes

Calories **55**
Protein **2g**
Cholesterol **0mg**
Total fat **4g**
Saturated fat **1g**
Sodium **125mg**

12.5 cl	unsalted veal or chicken stock	4 fl oz
2	sweet black peppers, seeded and deribbed, one coarsely chopped, the other very thinly sliced	2
1	dried hot red chili pepper, seeded and crushed (caution, page 17)	1
1	shallot, coarsely chopped	1
1½ tbsp	red wine vinegar	1½ tbsp
¾ tsp	sugar	¾ tsp
¼ tsp	salt	¼ tsp
	freshly ground black pepper	
1½ tbsp	virgin olive oil	1½ tbsp
1 tbsp	fresh lime juice	1 tbsp
1	large Batavian endive (about 750 g/ ½ lb), trimmed, cut in half through core	1

In a small frying pan, combine the stock, the chopped sweet pepper, chili pepper, shallot, vinegar, sugar, salt and some pepper. Simmer over low heat, stirring frequently, until only about 3 tablespoons of liquid remain — 7 to 10 minutes.

Transfer the contents of the pan to a blender. Add the oil and lime juice and purée the mixture to obtain a smooth dressing. Transfer the dressing to a large bowl; immediately add the sliced sweet pepper. Refrigerate the dressing until it is cool — about 15 minutes.

Lay an endive half on a work surface cut side down and slice it into chiffonade (*page 51*). Repeat the process with the other half. Toss the chiffonade with the dressing and serve the salad at once.

Gingery Cauliflower Salad

Serves 4 as a first course or side dish
Working time: about 20 minutes
Total time: about 45 minutes

Calories **60**
Protein **1g**
Cholesterol **0mg**
Total fat **4g**
Saturated fat **0g**
Sodium **150mg**

1	cauliflower, trimmed and cut into florets	1
2.5 cm	piece fresh ginger root, peeled and julienned	1 inch
1	carrot, julienned	1
2 tbsp	white vinegar	2 tbsp
½ tsp	sugar	½ tsp
¼ tsp	salt	¼ tsp
⅛ tsp	cayenne pepper	⅛ tsp
1 tbsp	safflower oil	1 tbsp
¼ tsp	dark sesame oil	¼ tsp
1	spring onion, trimmed, green part julienned and soaked in iced water, white part sliced diagonally into thin ovals	1

Mound the cauliflower florets on a heatproof plate to resemble a whole head of cauliflower. Scatter the ginger and carrot julienne over the cauliflower.

Combine the vinegar, sugar, salt and cayenne pepper in a small bowl. Whisk in the safflower oil and pour the dressing over the cauliflower.

Pour enough water into a large pan to fill it about 2.5 cm (1 inch) deep. Stand two or three small heatproof bowls in the water and set the plate with the cauliflower on top of the bowls. Cover the pan, bring the water to the boil and steam the cauliflower until it can be easily pierced with a knife — 15 to 20 minutes.

Remove the lid and let the steam dissipate. Lift the plate out of the pan and let the cauliflower stand until it cools to room temperature. Dribble the sesame oil over the cauliflower and scatter the green and white spring onion on top. Serve the salad at room temperature or chilled.

Sprouted Three-Bean Salad

ALTHOUGH SPROUTED MUNG BEANS ARE WIDELY AVAILABLE, SPROUTED CHICK-PEAS AND PINTO BEANS ARE NOT. TO SPROUT YOUR OWN, USE THE TECHNIQUE DESCRIBED OPPOSITE AND CONSULT THE TABLE FOR SPROUTING TIMES.

Serves 4 as a side dish
Working time: about 15 minutes
Total time: about 1 hour and 25 minutes (includes chilling)

Calories **80**
Protein **3g**
Cholesterol **0mg**
Total fat **4g**
Saturated fat **0g**
Sodium **180mg**

45 g	sweet green pepper, chopped	1½ oz
30 g	red onion, thinly sliced	1 oz
1	garlic clove, finely chopped	1
2 tbsp	chopped fresh basil, or 2 tsp dried basil	2 tbsp
2 tbsp	white vinegar	2 tbsp
2 tsp	sugar	2 tsp
¼ tsp	salt	¼ tsp
	freshly ground black pepper	
60 g	sprouted chick-peas	2 oz
60 g	sprouted pinto beans	2 oz
75 g	sprouted mung beans	2½ oz
1 tbsp	safflower oil	1 tbsp
1	lettuce, washed and dried	1

Bring two pans of water to the boil.

In a small bowl, combine the green pepper, onion, garlic, basil, vinegar, sugar, salt and some pepper. Set the mixture aside for at least 5 minutes.

Combine the sprouted chick-peas and pinto beans, and blanch them in one of the pans of boiling water until they are tender — 5 to 7 minutes. Blanch the sprouted mung beans in the other pan until they too are tender — 2 to 3 minutes. Drain all of the beans, rinse them under cold running water, drain again, and toss them together in a bowl.

Add the oil to the vinegar mixture and stir it in well. Pour the dressing over the sprouted beans and stir to coat them. Chill the salad for 1 hour in the refrigerator before serving it on a bed of lettuce.

A Home-Grown Treat

Sprouts, the germinated seeds of grains, legumes and other plants, constitute a welcome, crunchy addition to some salads — especially in winter, when the choice of fresh vegetables may be limited. Moreover, they pack a great deal of nutrition. During the sprouting process, the A, B, C and E vitamins they contain actually increase.

The range of seeds that may be sprouted is large indeed. Eight types are depicted here, including chick-peas, mung beans, and alfalfa and radish seeds, all called for by recipes in this book. When selecting seeds, choose only those that have been produced for consumption, not the garden variety, which may have been chemically treated.

Sprouts are so easy to germinate and take up so little space it is a wonder more people do not grow their own. All that is needed are the seeds, a container, and enough warmth and moisture for germination to occur. A sprouter like the compartmentalized one shown here allows for staggered sprouting times, guaranteeing a constant supply, or the production of several varieties at once. A large, wide-mouthed jar also works well.

If you pursue the jar method, drop in about ½ cup of the larger seeds or 2 or 3 tablespoons of the smaller ones. Add cold water in a ratio of about 4 parts water to 1 part seeds. Soak the larger seeds for 8 to 10 hours; the smaller ones may need only 3 to 6 hours (chart, right). Once the soaking is over, drain off the water and rinse the seeds well. Cover the mouth of the jar with muslin or mesh to allow air to enter and circulate, and gently shake the jar to distribute the seeds. Leave the jar in a warm, dark place, propped mouth down at a slight angle so that moisture can drain. Two or three times a day, fill the jar with cold water, gently swirl the contents, then drain them thoroughly.

Once the sprouts develop, they may be eaten at once or refrigerated, loosely packed in a covered container or a plastic bag, for up to five days. For added nutrition, you may wish to place sprouts bearing two little leaves in indirect light for several hours so that the leaves can turn green.

Sprouts await inclusion in salads. At the top, clockwise from right: kidney, fenugreek, chick-pea and azuki sprouts. At the bottom, clockwise from lower right: buckwheat, clover and radish sprouts. Mung beans spill from a bag; sprouted mung beans fill the jar.

A Sprouting Guide

	Soaking time (hours)	Sprouting time (days)	Sprout length (mm/inches)
Alfalfa	3-6	3-5	25-50 / 1-2
Azuki bean	5-10	2-4	10-35 / ½-1½
Buckwheat	4-8	2-3	5-10 / ¼-½
Chick-pea	8-12	2-4	10 / ½
Clover	3-6	3-6	25-50 / 1-2
Fenugreek	4-8	3-6	25-50 / 1-2
Kidney bean	8-12	2-4	10-25 / ½-1
Lentil	5-8	2-4	5-25 / ¼-1
Mung bean	5-10	3-5	25-50 / 1-2
Pinto bean	8-12	3-4	10-30 / ½-1¼
Radish	4-8	3-5	10-50 / ½-2

While the beans are cooking, prepare the dressing: combine the vinegar and soy sauce in a small bowl. Whisk in the oils, then the chili pepper, ginger, garlic and some black pepper.

Pour all but 2 tablespoons of the dressing over the sweet potatoes and beans; add the spring onions and toss well. Chill the vegetables for at least 1 hour.

To serve the salad, toss the cabbage with the remaining 2 tablespoons of dressing and transfer it to a serving plate. Mound the chilled vegetables on top and scatter the peanuts over all.

Sweet Potato Salad with Peanuts

Serves 8 as a side dish
Working time: about 30 minutes
Total time: about 1 hour and 30 minutes

Calories **150**
Protein **4g**
Cholesterol **0mg**
Total fat **4g**
Saturated fat **0g**
Sodium **140mg**

750 g	sweet potatoes, peeled, halved lengthwise and cut into 5 mm (¼ inch) thick slices	1½ lb
250 g	French beans, trimmed and cut in half	8 oz
3	spring onions, trimmed and thinly sliced	3
750 g	Chinese cabbage, sliced into chiffonade (page 51)	1½ lb
2 tbsp	coarsely chopped dry-roasted unsalted peanuts	2 tbsp
Ginger dressing		
4 tbsp	rice vinegar	4 tbsp
1 tbsp	low-sodium soy sauce or shoyu	1 tbsp
1 tbsp	safflower oil	1 tbsp
1 tsp	dark sesame oil	1 tsp
1	hot green chili pepper, seeded, deribbed and finely chopped (caution, page 17)	1
1 tbsp	finely chopped fresh ginger root	1 tbsp
1	garlic clove, finely chopped	1
	freshly ground black pepper	

To cook the sweet potatoes, pour enough water into a saucepan to fill it about 2.5 cm (1 inch) deep. Set a steamer in the pan and bring the water to the boil. Put the sweet potatoes into the steamer, cover the pan tightly, and steam the sweet potatoes until they are just tender — about 10 minutes. Transfer the sweet potatoes to a large bowl and set them aside.

Steam the beans until they are cooked but still crisp — about 4 minutes. Refresh the beans under cold running water to preserve their colour, then add them to the bowl with the sweet potatoes.

Artichoke Bottoms in Mango and Red Onion Dressing

Serves 6 as a first course or side dish
Working time: about 40 minutes
Total time: about 1 hour

Calories **70**
Protein **1g**
Cholesterol **0mg**
Total fat **2g**
Saturated fat **0g**
Sodium **75mg**

8	large globe artichokes	8
1	lemon, cut in half	1
1	ripe mango, peeled, the flesh cut into small cubes	1
1½ tbsp	fresh lemon or lime juice	1½ tbsp
1 tbsp	red wine vinegar	1 tbsp
1 tbsp	virgin olive oil	1 tbsp
⅛ tsp	salt	⅛ tsp
	freshly ground black pepper	
60 g	red onion, chopped	2 oz

To prepare the artichoke bottoms, first break or cut the stem off one of the artichokes. Snap off and discard the outer leaves, starting at the base and continuing until you reach the pale yellow leaves at the core. Cut the top two thirds off the artichoke. Trim away any dark green leaf bases that remain on the artichoke bottom. Rub the artichoke all over with a lemon half to keep it from discolouring. Repeat these steps to prepare the remaining artichoke bottoms.

Heat 12.5 cl (4 fl oz) of water in a large, non-reactive sauté pan over low heat. Put the artichoke bottoms into the water, tightly cover the pan, and steam them for 7 minutes. Turn them over, cover the pan again, and continue steaming until tender when pierced with a knife —about 7 minutes more. Transfer the artichokes to a plate and refrigerate them.

While the artichokes are cooking, prepare the dressing. Put the mango, lemon or lime juice, vinegar, oil, salt and some pepper into a food processor or blender. Purée the mixture, scraping down the sides at least once during the process. Transfer the dressing to a large bowl and stir in the onion.

When the artichokes are cool, scrape out the chokes with a spoon. Cut each artichoke into 12 wedges and stir them into the mango dressing. Chill the salad for at least 10 minutes before serving it.

Endive Salad with Orange and Rosemary

Serves 6 as a first course or side dish
Working (and total) time: about 25 minutes

Calories **70**
Protein **2g**
Cholesterol **0mg**
Total fat **4g**
Saturated fat **1g**
Sodium **105mg**

1	garlic clove, cut in half	1
1	head of curly endive, washed and dried	1
3	small heads of chicory, washed, dried and sliced crosswise into 1 cm (½ inch) wide strips	3
1	navel orange	1
1	small red onion, thinly sliced	1
1 tbsp	chopped fresh rosemary, or 1 tsp dried rosemary, crumbled	1 tbsp
⅛ tsp	salt	⅛ tsp
2 tbsp	sherry vinegar or red wine vinegar	2 tbsp
1 tbsp	grainy mustard	1 tbsp
1½ tbsp	virgin olive oil	1½ tbsp

Rub the inside of a salad bowl with the cut surfaces of the garlic clove. Put the endive and chicory into the bowl. Working over a bowl to catch the juice, cut away the peel, white pith and outer membrane from the flesh of the orange. To separate the segments from the membranes, slice down to the core with a sharp knife on either side of each segment and set the segments aside. Cut each segment in thirds and add them to the bowl along with the onion and rosemary.

In a small bowl, whisk together the salt, reserved orange juice, vinegar and mustard. Whisking constantly, pour in the oil in a thin, steady stream to create an emulsified dressing. Pour the dressing over the contents of the salad bowl; toss the salad thoroughly and serve it at once.

Chicory and Watercress Salad

Serves 6 as a first course or side dish
Working (and total) time: about 30 minutes

Calories **70**
Protein **2g**
Cholesterol **0mg**
Total fat **5g**
Saturated fat **1g**
Sodium **140mg**

2	heads of chicory	2
1	bunch watercress, stemmed, washed and dried	1
12	mushrooms, stems trimmed, caps wiped clean and thinly sliced	12
18	cherry tomatoes, halved	18
Dill-mustard vinaigrette		
1 tbsp	herb-flavoured mustard or Dijon mustard	1 tbsp
2 tbsp	finely cut fresh dill, or 1½ tbsp dried dill	2 tbsp
3	spring onions, trimmed, green parts reserved for another use, white parts finely chopped	3
1½ tbsp	fresh lemon juice	1½ tbsp
¼ tsp	salt	¼ tsp
	freshly ground black pepper	
1 tbsp	safflower oil	1 tbsp
1 tbsp	virgin olive oil	1 tbsp

To make the vinaigrette, combine the mustard, dill, spring onions, lemon juice, salt and some pepper in a small bowl. Whisking vigorously, pour in the safflower oil in a thin, steady stream; incorporate the olive oil the same way. Set the vinaigrette aside.

Separate the chicory leaves from their cores. Arrange the chicory leaves, watercress, mushrooms and tomatoes on individual plates. Spoon the vinaigrette over the salad and serve immediately.

Brussels Sprouts in Basil-Yogurt Dressing

THE TECHNIQUE OF SCULPTING VEGETABLES IN THE SHAPE OF
SMALL MUSHROOMS IS DEMONSTRATED OPPOSITE

Serves 4 as a first course or side dish
Working time: about 25 minutes
Total time: about 1 hour

Calories **85**
Protein **4g**
Cholesterol **2mg**
Total fat **1g**
Saturated fat **1g**
Sodium **75mg**

350 g	Brussels sprouts, quartered	12 oz
250 g	swedes, cut into mushrooms, the mushrooms sliced in half	8 oz
2	turnips, cut into mushrooms, the mushrooms sliced in half	2
	Basil-yogurt dressing	
2 tbsp	sweet sherry	2 tbsp
1	garlic clove, finely chopped	1
1 tbsp	chopped fresh basil, or 1 tsp dried basil	1 tbsp
1 tsp	Dijon mustard	1 tsp
6 tbsp	plain low-fat yogurt	6 tbsp
2 tsp	soured cream	2 tsp
1 tbsp	finely chopped spring onion	1 tbsp
	white pepper	
	several radicchio or cos lettuce leaves, washed and dried	

Pour enough water into a saucepan to fill it about 2.5 cm (1 inch) deep. Set a vegetable steamer in the pan and bring the water to the boil. Put the Brussels sprouts into the steamer, cover the pan tightly, and steam the sprouts until they are tender — about 5 minutes. Transfer the sprouts to a large bowl and set them aside. Steam the swede and turnip mushrooms until they are tender — 6 to 7 minutes — and transfer them to the bowl with the Brussels sprouts.

While the vegetables are steaming, prepare the dressing. Combine the sherry, garlic and basil in a small saucepan. Simmer the mixture over medium heat until only 1 tablespoon of liquid remains — 2 to 3 minutes. Transfer the mixture to a small bowl; stir in the mustard, then the yogurt, soured cream, spring onion and some white pepper.

Pour the dressing over the vegetables and toss the mixture well. Cover the bowl and chill the salad for about 20 minutes. Mound the salad on the radicchio or lettuce leaves just before serving.

Making "Mushrooms" from Root Vegetables

1 *SCOOPING OUT ROUNDS. Slice the top and bottom off the vegetable (here, a swede) and pare it. With a large melon baller, dig deeply into the edge and scoop out as many rounds as the vegetable will yield.*

2 *INSERTING THE CORER. To make the stem, place a round on the work surface with the flat end upturned. Push the cutting edge of a fruit corer into the centre of the flat end, about 1 cm (½ inch) deep.*

3 *TRIMMING THE PIECE. With the round still attached to the corer, cut through to the corer with a paring knife. Slowly rotating the corer, hold the knife in place until a cut has been made round the piece.*

4 *SEPARATING THE MUSHROOM. Carefully separate the cut piece from the round by prising it loose with the knife blade. Then grip the top of the round with your fingertips and pull out the mushroom.*

Broccoli and Chinese Cabbage Salad with Black Vinegar Dressing

Serves 8 as a side dish
Working (and total) time: about 25 minutes

Calories **40**
Protein **2g**
Cholesterol **0mg**
Total fat **2g**
Saturated fat **0g**
Sodium **120mg**

2	broccoli stalks, florets separated from stems, stems peeled and sliced diagonally	2
1	daikon radish (mooli)	1
300 g	Chinese cabbage, sliced into 1 cm (½ inch) pieces	10 oz
1 tbsp	safflower oil	1 tbsp
¼ tsp	dark sesame oil	¼ tsp
	Black vinegar dressing	
½ litre	unsalted chicken stock	16 fl oz
4	thin slices peeled fresh ginger root	4
1 tsp	Sichuan peppercorns	1 tsp
¼ tsp	sugar	¼ tsp
2 tbsp	Chinese black vinegar or balsamic vinegar	2 tbsp
1 tbsp	low-sodium soy sauce or shoyu	1 tbsp

To make the dressing, first pour the stock into a small saucepan set over medium-high heat. Add the ginger, peppercorns and sugar, and bring the liquid to the boil. Cook the mixture until it is reduced to about 12.5 cl (4 fl oz) — 10 to 12 minutes.

While the stock is reducing, cook the broccoli. Pour enough water into a saucepan to fill it about 2.5 cm (1 inch) deep. Set a vegetable steamer in the water and add the broccoli florets and stems. Cover the pan tightly, bring the water to the boil, and steam the broccoli until it is barely tender — about 2 minutes. Transfer the broccoli to a bowl and refrigerate it until serving time.

Remove the reduced stock from the heat and let it cool. Stir in the vinegar and soy sauce, then strain the dressing into a small serving bowl.

Slice the daikon radish into 5 cm (2 inch) lengths. Stand one of the pieces on end; using a small, sharp knife, cut down the sides to remove the peel, giving the radish five sides. Repeat the process to fashion the remaining radish pieces. Thinly slice the pieces; keep them in iced water until serving time.

Drain the radish slices, pat them dry with paper towels, and transfer them to a large bowl along with the broccoli and cabbage. Combine the safflower oil and sesame oil; dribble the oils over the vegetables, toss well and serve. Pass the dressing separately.

Sweet Potato Salad with Curried Yogurt Dressing

Serves 6 as a side dish
Working time: about 30 minutes
Total time: about 2 hours (includes chilling)

Calories **120**
Protein **3g**
Cholesterol **2mg**
Total fat **1g**
Saturated fat **0g**
Sodium **60mg**

500 g	sweet potatoes	1 lb
4	sticks celery, thinly sliced	4
3	spring onions, trimmed and thinly sliced	3
12.5 cl	yogurt dressing (recipe, page 13) mixed with 1 ½ tsp curry powder	4 fl oz
1 tbsp	each finely cut chives and chopped parsley, or 2 tbsp chopped parsley	1 tbsp

Put the sweet potatoes in a deep saucepan and pour in enough water to cover them. Bring the water to the boil and cook the sweet potatoes over medium heat until they are tender — 25 to 30 minutes. Drain the sweet potatoes; when they are cool enough to handle, peel them and cut them into small dice. Put the sweet potatoes in a bowl with the celery and spring onions.

Add the dressing to the vegetables and mix gently. Chill the salad for at least 1 hour. Just before serving, sprinkle the fresh herbs over the top.

EDITOR'S NOTE: *This salad makes a delicious accompaniment to grilled chicken or pork.*

Chayote Fans in a Coriander Vinaigrette

Serves 4 as a first course
Working time: about 25 minutes
Total time: about 45 minutes

Calories **60**
Protein **1g**
Cholesterol **0mg**
Total fat **4g**
Saturated fat **0g**
Sodium **80mg**

1	large chayote (about 350 g/12 oz), quartered and seeded	1
1	lemon	1
1 tbsp	red wine vinegar	1 tbsp
½ tsp	Dijon mustard	½ tsp
1 tbsp	safflower oil	1 tbsp
1 tbsp	chopped fresh coriander	1 tbsp
½ tsp	sugar	½ tsp
⅛ tsp	salt	⅛ tsp
	freshly ground black pepper	
1	large dried mild chili pepper, cut in half lengthwise and seeded	1
4	fresh coriander sprigs for garnish	4

Cut a chayote quarter lengthwise into thin slices, leaving the slices attached at the tapered end to form a fan. Repeat the process with the other quarters.

Pour enough water into a saucepan to fill it about 2.5 cm (1 inch) deep. Set a vegetable steamer in the pan and bring the water to the boil. Set the chayote fans in the steamer, cover the pan, and steam the vegetable until it is barely tender — 4 to 5 minutes. Transfer the chayote to a shallow bowl.

Cut the lemon in half. Slice one half into four rounds and reserve the rounds for garnish. Squeeze enough juice from the other half to measure 1 tablespoon and pour it into a small mixing bowl. Add the vinegar and mustard, and whisk in the oil. Season the vinaigrette with the coriander, sugar, salt and some pepper. Pour the vinaigrette over the chayote fans and chill them.

Meanwhile, place the chili pepper in a small bowl, pour ¼ litre (8 fl oz) of boiling water over it, and let it soak for 20 minutes. Remove the chili pepper from its soaking liquid; do not discard the liquid. Put the pepper pieces in a blender along with 4 tablespoons of the soaking liquid. Drain the vinaigrette from the chilled chayote and add it to the pepper pieces and liquid. Purée the dressing and strain it through a fine sieve.

Spoon the dressing on to four individual salad plates. Transfer the chayote fans to the plates and place a sprig of coriander on each fan. Garnish each salad with a lemon round.

Courgette and Apple in Rice Vinegar

Serves 8 as a side dish
Working (and total) time: about 20 minutes

Calories **30**
Protein **1g**
Cholesterol **0mg**
Total fat **1g**
Saturated fat **0g**
Sodium **35mg**

250 g	courgettes, julienned	8 oz
1	green apple, peeled, cored, julienned	1
1	red apple, quartered, cored, thinly sliced	1
1 tsp	chopped fresh tarragon, or ½ tsp dried tarragon	1 tsp
1 tsp	safflower oil	1 tsp
2 tbsp	rice vinegar	2 tbsp
⅛ tsp	salt	⅛ tsp
	freshly ground black pepper	

In a large bowl, combine the courgettes, apples and tarragon. Add the oil and toss the mixture to coat the salad. Stir in the vinegar, salt and some pepper; toss the salad and serve it at once.

Kohlrabi Salad

Serves 6 as a side dish
Working (and total) time: about 40 minutes

Calories **45**
Protein **3g**
Cholesterol **3mg**
Total fat **2g**
Saturated fat **0g**
Sodium **45mg**

500 g	kohlrabies or turnips, peeled and shredded	1 lb
4 tbsp	diced pimiento	4 tbsp
1 tbsp	fresh lemon juice	1 tbsp
12.5 cl	yogurt dressing (recipe, page 13)	4 fl oz

Pour 2 litres (3½ pints) of cold water into a saucepan. Add the kohlrabi or turnip shreds, bring the water to the boil, then blanch for 2 minutes. Drain them in a colander, refresh them under cold running water, and drain them again. Rid the vegetables of excess moisture by pressing down on them with the back of a large spoon. (Or wrap them in muslin and wring out.)

Transfer the kohlrabi or turnip shreds to a bowl and stir in the pimiento and lemon juice. Pour the dressing over the top, toss the salad well, and serve it at once.

Sautéed Greens with Red Potatoes and Apple

Serves 8 as a side dish
Working time: about 25 minutes
Total time: about 1 hour and 25 minutes

Calories **105**
Protein **2g**
Cholesterol **2mg**
Total fat **3g**
Saturated fat **1g**
Sodium **150mg**

1	large tart apple	1
1 tbsp	fresh lemon juice	1 tbsp
500 g	red potatoes, scrubbed and cut into 2 cm (¾ inch) cubes	1 lb
½ tsp	salt	½ tsp
1 tbsp	red wine vinegar	1 tbsp
1½ tbsp	virgin olive oil	1½ tbsp
1	shallot, finely chopped	1
250 g	spinach, spring greens, Swiss chard leaves or young kale, stemmed, washed, torn into 5 cm (2 inch) pieces and dried	8 oz
12.5 cl	milk	4 fl oz
	freshly ground black pepper	

Peel, quarter and core the apple, and cut it into 2 cm (¾ inch) pieces. In a small bowl, toss the apple with the lemon juice; set the bowl aside.

Pour ½ litre (16 fl oz) of water into a saucepan. Add the potatoes and salt, and bring the water to the boil. Reduce the heat and simmer the potatoes for 10 minutes. Add the apple to the saucepan and continue cooking the mixture, stirring often so that it does not burn, until only 2 tablespoons of liquid remain — about 10 minutes more.

Combine the wine vinegar and ½ tablespoon of the olive oil in a small bowl. Pour this mixture over the hot potatoes and apple, and set them aside.

Heat the remaining oil in a large, heavy frying pan over medium heat. Cook the shallot in the oil for 1 minute. Add the greens and cook them, stirring frequently, until they are wilted — about 3 minutes. Pour in the milk and continue cooking the mixture until all the liquid has evaporated — 7 to 10 minutes.

Combine the potato mixture, the greens and a generous grinding of pepper in a large bowl. Toss the salad well and refrigerate it for at least 45 minutes. Toss it once more before serving.

French Beans with Creamy Horseradish Dressing

Serves 8 as a first course
Working time: about 40 minutes
Total time: about 1 hour and 15 minutes

Calories **55**
Protein **3g**
Cholesterol **1mg**
Total fat **1g**
Saturated fat **0g**
Sodium **115mg**

2	sweet red peppers	2
8	globe artichokes	8
1	lemon, halved	1
250 g	French beans, trimmed	8 oz
250 g	okra, trimmed	8 oz
Horseradish dressing		
12.5 cl	plain low-fat yogurt	4 fl oz
4 tbsp	grated horseradish	4 tbsp
1 tsp	celery seeds	1 tsp
1 tsp	fresh lemon juice	1 tsp
¼ tsp	salt	¼ tsp
1 tbsp	chopped fresh thyme, or 1 tsp dried thyme	1 tbsp
3 tbsp	chopped parsley	3 tbsp
⅛ tsp	cayenne pepper	⅛ tsp
	freshly ground black pepper	

Roast the peppers about 5 cm (2 inches) below a pre-heated grill, turning them until the skins have blistered on all sides. Transfer the peppers to a bowl and cover it with plastic film; the trapped steam will loosen the skins. When the peppers are cool enough to handle, peel, seed and derib them, and cut them into 5 mm (¼ inch) cubes.

To prepare each artichoke bottom, first break or cut off the stem. Snap off and discard the outer leaves, starting at the base and continuing until you reach the pale yellow leaves at the core. Cut the top two thirds off the artichoke. Trim away any dark green leaf bases that remain on the artichoke bottom. Rub the artichoke all over with one of the lemon halves.

Fill a large, non-reactive saucepan with water and bring it to the boil. Squeeze the juice of both lemon halves into the water, then add the lemon halves themselves. Add the artichoke bottoms to the boiling water and cook them until they can be easily pierced with the tip of a sharp knife — about 15 minutes. Drain the artichoke bottoms and refresh them under cold running water. Using a teaspoon, scrape the furry choke from each artichoke bottom. Rinse and drain the bottoms, and cut each one into eight pieces.

Pour enough water into a large saucepan to fill it about 2.5 cm (1 inch) deep. Set a vegetable steamer in the pan and bring the water to the boil. Put the French beans into the steamer, cover the pan tightly, and steam the beans until they are tender — about 6 minutes. Lift out the steamer; refresh the beans under cold running water, then drain them well, and set them aside.

Return the steamer to the pan and bring the water to the boil. Set the okra in the steamer, cover the pan tightly, and steam the okra until it is barely tender — about 3 minutes. Remove the okra from the pan and refresh it under cold running water. Cut each okra in half lengthwise and set it aside.

To prepare the dressing, whisk together the yogurt, horseradish, celery seeds, lemon juice, salt, thyme, parsley, cayenne pepper and some black pepper in a large bowl. Add the beans, artichoke bottoms, okra and all but 2 tablespoons of the red peppers to the dressing. Toss well and serve the salad with the reserved red pepper cubes sprinkled on top.

EDITOR'S NOTE: *Provided it is stored in the refrigerator, the dressing may be made a day in advance.*

Carrot and Orange Salad with Dill

Serves 4 as a side dish
Working time: about 10 minutes
Total time: about 25 minutes

Calories **90**
Protein **2g**
Cholesterol **0mg**
Total fat **0g**
Saturated fat **0g**
Sodium **50mg**

1	large juicy orange	1
600 g	carrots, finely grated	1¼ lb
1 tbsp	red wine vinegar	1 tbsp
12.5 cl	fresh orange juice	4 fl oz
½ tsp	grated orange rind	½ tsp
2 tbsp	fresh dill	2 tbsp

Working over a bowl to catch the juice, cut away the peel, white pith and outer membrane from the orange. To separate the segments from the inner membranes, slice down to the core with a sharp knife on either side of each segment and set the segments aside.

Combine the carrots, vinegar, orange juice and rind in the bowl. Add the orange segments and 1 tablespoon of the dill; gently toss the ingredients. Refrigerate the salad for at least 15 minutes. Shortly before serving, garnish the top with the remaining dill.

Red, White and Green Salad

Serves 6 as a first course or side dish
Working time: about 20 minutes
Total time: about 1 hour

Calories **60**
Protein **2g**
Cholesterol **0mg**
Total fat **4g**
Saturated fat **0g**
Sodium **75mg**

250 g	beetroot, rinsed	8 oz
3 tbsp	raspberry vinegar or red wine vinegar	3 tbsp
2 tsp	Dijon mustard	2 tsp
2 tsp	grainy mustard	2 tsp
¼ tsp	honey	¼ tsp
	freshly ground black pepper	
1 ½ tbsp	virgin olive oil	1 ½ tbsp
1	head of radicchio, halved, cored, washed, dried and cut into chiffonade (opposite)	1
1	large head of chicory, cored, cut in half crosswise, the halves julienned	1
125 g	lamb's lettuce (corn salad or mâche), washed and dried, or 1 small lettuce, washed, dried and torn into pieces	4 oz

Put the beetroot into a saucepan, pour in enough water to cover, and bring the water to the boil. Cook the beetroot until it is tender — about 30 minutes. Drain the beetroot and let it cool before peeling and

finely dicing it. Put the diced beetroot in a small bowl, and toss it with 1 tablespoon of the vinegar.

To make the dressing, combine the mustards, the honey, the remaining vinegar and a liberal grinding of pepper in a bowl. Whisk in the oil.

In another bowl, toss the radicchio and chicory with two thirds of the dressing. Separately toss the lamb's lettuce with the remaining dressing.

To assemble the salad, mound the radicchio-chicory mixture in the centre of a platter and surround it with the lettuce. Scatter the diced beetroot on top.

Cutting Chiffonade

1 ROLLING THE LEAVES. Pluck the leaves from a head of spinach, cabbage or lettuce (here, radicchio). Gently wash and dry the leaves. Stack three to four leaves and roll them into a bundle.

2 CUTTING THE ROLL. Holding the bundle with your fingers curled under for safety, square the end by cutting off the rounded tips of the leaves. Slice across the roll at approximately 3 mm (⅛ inch) intervals to produce the thin strips called chiffonade.

Spinach and Sesame Salad

Serves 6 as a side dish
Working (and total) time: about 30 minutes

Calories **60**
Protein **4g**
Cholesterol **0mg**
Total fat **5g**
Saturated fat **0g**
Sodium **255mg**

12.5 cl	unsalted chicken stock	4 fl oz
1 tbsp	sesame seeds	1 tbsp
1 tbsp	tahini (sesame paste)	1 tbsp
1 tsp	dark sesame oil	1 tsp
1½ tbsp	low-sodium soy sauce or shoyu	1½ tbsp
1 tbsp	fresh lemon juice	1 tbsp
1 tsp	finely chopped fresh ginger root	1 tsp
500 g	spinach, washed, stemmed and dried	1 lb
125 g	mushrooms, wiped clean and thinly sliced	4 oz
1	large ripe tomato, sliced into thin wedges	1
⅛ tsp	salt	⅛ tsp
	freshly ground black pepper	

Boil the stock in a small saucepan until only 2 tablespoons remain — about 7 minutes.

While the stock is reducing, toast the sesame seeds in a small, heavy frying pan over medium-low heat until they are golden — about 3 minutes. Set the pan aside.

To prepare the dressing, mix the tahini and sesame oil in a small bowl. Whisk in the reduced stock, the soy sauce, lemon juice and ginger.

Put the spinach and mushrooms into a large bowl. Sprinkle the tomato wedges with the salt and pepper and add them to the bowl. Pour the dressing over the vegetables, grind in some more pepper, and toss well. Scatter the sesame seeds over the salad and serve.

Kale, Pear and Goat Cheese Salad

Serves 8 as a first course
Working (and total) time: about 40 minutes

Calories **90**
Protein **4g**
Cholesterol **5mg**
Total fat **4g**
Saturated fat **1g**
Sodium **200mg**

1½ tbsp	virgin olive oil	1½ tbsp
500 g	onions, thinly sliced	1 lb
¼ tsp	salt	¼ tsp
500 g	kale, stemmed and washed, large leaves torn in half	1 lb
12.5 cl	cider vinegar	4 fl oz
60 g	thinly sliced pancetta (Italian bacon) or prosciutto, cut into thin strips	2 oz
1	pear, quartered, cored and thinly sliced lengthwise	1
	freshly ground black pepper	
60 g	fresh goat cheese, broken into small pieces	2 oz

Heat 1 tablespoon of the olive oil in a large, heavy frying pan over medium heat. Add the onions and ⅛ teaspoon of the salt; cook the onions, scraping the browned bits from the bottom of the pan vigorously and often, until the onions are caramelized — 25 to 30 minutes.

Meanwhile, cook the kale in 3 litres (5 pints) of boiling water for 7 minutes. Drain the kale and refresh it under cold running water. When the kale has cooled thoroughly, mould it into a ball and squeeze out as much liquid as possible.

When the onions are caramelized, stir the vinegar into the pan, scraping up any remaining pan deposits. Continue cooking the mixture until most of the liquid has evaporated — about 5 minutes.

Heat the remaining oil in a smaller frying pan over medium heat. Cook the pancetta or prosciutto in the oil for 1 minute, add it to the onion mixture, then stir in the kale, the sliced pear, the remaining salt and a generous grinding of black pepper. Stir in half of the goat cheese.

Divide the mixture among eight plates; dot the tops of the portions with the remaining cheese and serve the salad immediately.

Chilled Celeriac, Carrot and Yellow Pepper Salad

Serves 6 as a side dish
Working time: about 15 minutes
Total time: about 1 hour and 15 minutes

Calories **45**
Protein **1g**
Cholesterol **0mg**
Total fat **2g**
Saturated fat **0g**
Sodium **90mg**

250 g	celeriac, scrubbed	8 oz
2 tbsp	red wine vinegar	2 tbsp
1	carrot, peeled and julienned	1
1	sweet yellow pepper, seeded, deribbed and cut into thin strips	1
1 tbsp	safflower oil	1 tbsp
¼ tsp	sugar	¼ tsp
⅛ tsp	salt	⅛ tsp

Peel and julienne the celeriac. To prevent discoloration, transfer the pieces to a bowl and sprinkle them with the vinegar; toss the pieces well to coat them. Add the carrot, yellow pepper, oil, sugar and salt, and toss thoroughly to combine all the ingredients. Cover and refrigerate for at least 1 hour before serving.

Lettuce Leaves in a Garlicky Vinaigrette

Serves 6 as a first course or side dish
Working time: about 10 minutes
Total time: about 25 minutes

Calories **110**
Protein **3g**
Cholesterol **0mg**
Total fat **5g**
Saturated fat **1g**
Sodium **150mg**

1	whole garlic bulb, the cloves separated and peeled	1
1 tbsp	balsamic vinegar, or ¾ tbsp red wine vinegar mixed with ¼ tsp honey	1 tbsp
1 tbsp	virgin olive oil	1 tbsp
1 tbsp	safflower oil	1 tbsp
⅛ tsp	salt	⅛ tsp
	freshly ground black pepper	
2	large round lettuces, leaves washed and dried	2
12	thin French bread slices, toasted	12

Put the garlic cloves into a small saucepan and pour in enough water to cover them. Bring the liquid to the boil, then reduce the heat, and simmer the garlic until it is quite tender — about 15 minutes. Increase the heat and boil the liquid until only about 2 tablespoons remain — 2 to 3 minutes.

Pour the contents of the saucepan into a sieve set over a small bowl. With a wooden spoon, mash the garlic through the sieve into the bowl. Whisk the vinegar into the garlic mixture, then incorporate the olive oil, safflower oil, salt and some pepper.

Toss the lettuce leaves with the dressing; garnish the salad with the toast and serve at once.

Potato Salad with Roasted Red Pepper Sauce

Serves 8 as a side dish
Working (and total) time: about 40 minutes

Calories **110**
Protein **2g**
Cholesterol **0mg**
Total fat **4g**
Saturated fat **0g**
Sodium **70mg**

750 g	round red potatoes or other waxy potatoes, scrubbed	1½ lb
2	sweet red peppers	2
2	garlic cloves, peeled and crushed	2
1 tsp	chopped fresh rosemary, or ½ tsp dried rosemary, crumbled	1 tsp
¼ tsp	salt	¼ tsp
	cayenne pepper	
2 tbsp	red wine vinegar	2 tbsp
2 tbsp	virgin olive oil	2 tbsp
175 g	rocket, washed and dried, or 2 bunches watercress, stemmed, washed and dried	6 oz

Put the potatoes into a large saucepan and cover them with cold water. Bring the water to the boil and cook the potatoes until they are tender when pierced with the tip of a sharp knife — about 25 minutes. Drain the potatoes and set them aside to cool.

While the potatoes are boiling, roast the peppers about 5 cm (2 inches) below a preheated grill, turning them often, until they are blistered on all sides. Put the peppers into a bowl and cover the bowl with plastic film; the trapped steam will loosen their skins. Peel the peppers, then seed and derib them. Put the peppers into a food processor or a blender along with the garlic, rosemary, salt and a pinch of cayenne pepper. Purée the mixture to obtain a smooth sauce. With the motor still running, pour in the vinegar, then the oil; continue blending the sauce until it is well combined.

Cut the potatoes in half and then into wedges. Arrange the wedges on a bed of rocket leaves or watercress. Pour some of the sauce over the potatoes and serve the rest alongside.

Grilled Aubergine with Mint

Serves 6 as a side dish
Working time: about 25 minutes
Total time: about 50 minutes

Calories **70**
Protein **2g**
Cholesterol **0mg**
Total fat **3g**
Saturated fat **0g**
Sodium **190mg**

500 g	aubergine, cut into 2.5 cm (1 inch) cubes	1 lb
½ tsp	salt	½ tsp
2 tbsp	balsamic vinegar, or 1½ tbsp red wine vinegar mixed with ½ tsp honey	2 tbsp
125 g	mushrooms, wiped clean and quartered	4 oz
½	lemon, juice only	½
2	ripe tomatoes, skinned, seeded and cut into strips	2
1 tbsp	sliced fresh mint leaves	1 tbsp
Peppery orange dressing		
1	orange, juice only	1
1	lemon, juice only	1
1	garlic clove, finely chopped	1
⅛ tsp	hot red pepper flakes	⅛ tsp
¼ tsp	salt	¼ tsp
1 tbsp	virgin olive oil	1 tbsp

Toss the aubergine cubes with the salt and let them stand for 30 minutes to make them less bitter. Rinse the cubes and pat them dry with paper towels.

Preheat the grill. Put the aubergine cubes into a fireproof dish and grill them, stirring often, until they are browned — about 5 minutes. Transfer them to a bowl and mix in the vinegar. Set the bowl aside.

Put the mushrooms into a non-reactive saucepan with the lemon juice; pour in enough water to cover the mushrooms and simmer them over medium heat for about 5 minutes. Set the saucepan aside.

To make the dressing, combine the orange juice, lemon juice, garlic, red pepper flakes and salt in a small saucepan. Bring the mixture to the boil and cook it until the liquid is reduced by half — about 5 minutes. Remove the pan from the heat and whisk in the oil.

Arrange the aubergine cubes and tomato strips on a large plate. Drain the mushrooms and scatter them over the top. Pour the dressing over the vegetables, then sprinkle the fresh mint on top. Serve the salad at room temperature.

Broad Bean Salad

Serves 6 as a first course or side dish
Working time: about 40 minutes
Total time: about 50 minutes

Calories **125**
Protein **6g**
Cholesterol **3mg**
Total fat **3g**
Saturated fat **1g**
Sodium **95mg**

2 tsp	virgin olive oil	2 tsp
1	large onion, thinly sliced	1
1	large garlic clove, finely chopped	1
1.25 kg	fresh broad beans, shelled and peeled, or 150 g (5 oz) frozen broad beans	2½ lb
30 g	paper-thin slices of prosciutto, julienned	1 oz
750 g	ripe tomatoes, skinned, seeded and coarsely chopped, or 400 g (14 oz) canned tomatoes, chopped, with juice	1½ lb
¼ litre	unsalted chicken stock, or 12.5 cl (4 fl oz) unsalted chicken stock if canned tomatoes are used	8 fl oz
1 tbsp	chopped fresh oregano, or 1 tsp dried oregano	1 tbsp
½ tsp	cracked black peppercorns	½ tsp
2 tbsp	balsamic vinegar, or 1½ tbsp red wine vinegar mixed with ½ tsp honey	2 tbsp

Heat the oil in a heavy frying pan over medium heat. Add the onion slices and cook them until they are translucent — 4 to 5 minutes. Stir in the garlic and cook the mixture for 1 minute more. Add the beans, prosciutto, tomatoes, stock, oregano and peppercorns. Bring the liquid to a simmer and cook the mixture until the beans are just tender — 8 to 10 minutes. Transfer to a bowl and refrigerate. When the salad is cool, pour in the vinegar, toss well and serve at once.

French Bean Salad with Gruyère and Grainy Mustard

Serves 6 as a first course or side dish
Working time: about 15 minutes
Total time: about 30 minutes

Calories **70**
Protein **3g**
Cholesterol **8mg**
Total fat **5g**
Saturated fat **2g**
Sodium **120mg**

350 g	French beans, trimmed, halved diagonally	12 oz
1	shallot, finely chopped	1
1½ tbsp	grainy mustard, or 1 tbsp Dijon mustard	1½ tbsp
3 tbsp	red wine vinegar	3 tbsp
1 tbsp	virgin olive oil	1 tbsp
⅛ tsp	salt	⅛ tsp
	freshly ground black pepper	
45 g	Gruyère cheese, julienned	1½ oz

Pour enough water into a large saucepan to fill it about 2.5 cm (1 inch) deep. Set a vegetable steamer in the pan and bring the water to the boil. Put the beans into the steamer, cover the pan, and cook the beans until they are just tender — 7 to 8 minutes. Refresh the beans under cold running water; when they are cool, drain them on paper towels.

Mix the shallot, mustard, vinegar, oil, salt and some pepper in a large bowl. Add the cheese and beans, and toss them well. Refrigerate the salad for 10 minutes. Toss it once again just before serving.

Summer Vegetables in Tomato Aspic

Serves 16 as a side dish
Working time: about 30 minutes
Total time: about 4 hours and 30 minutes
(includes chilling)

Calories **50**
Protein **3g**
Cholesterol **0mg**
Total fat **1g**
Saturated fat **0g**
Sodium **50mg**

250 g	fresh sweetcorn kernels (cut from 2 small ears), or frozen sweetcorn kernels, thawed	8 oz
800 g	canned tomatoes, puréed in a food processor or blender	28 oz
1	cucumber, seeded and chopped	1
½	sweet red pepper, seeded, deribbed and chopped	½
½	sweet green pepper, seeded, deribbed and chopped	½
1	small onion, finely chopped	1
1 tbsp	red wine vinegar	1 tbsp
1 tbsp	virgin olive oil	1 tbsp
6	drops Tabasco sauce	6
¼ tsp	celery seeds	¼ tsp
¼ tsp	salt	¼ tsp
	freshly ground black pepper	
2 tbsp	powdered gelatine	2 tbsp
35 cl	cold unsalted chicken or vegetable stock	12 fl oz
1	large round lettuce, washed and dried	1

If you are using fresh sweetcorn, pour enough water into a saucepan to fill it about 2.5 cm (1 inch) deep. Set a vegetable steamer in the pan and bring the water to the boil. Put the fresh sweetcorn into the steamer; frozen sweetcorn does not require steaming. Tightly cover the pan and steam the sweetcorn for 3 minutes.

In a large bowl, combine the puréed tomatoes, the cucumber, red and green pepper, onion, sweetcorn,

vinegar, oil, Tabasco sauce, celery seeds, salt and some pepper. Set the bowl aside.

Stir the gelatine into 12.5 cl (4 fl oz) of the stock and set the mixture aside for 1 to 2 minutes. Bring the remaining stock to the boil, then remove it from the heat; add the gelatine-stock mixture and stir until the gelatine is dissolved.

Add the gelatine and stock to the vegetables and stir well to distribute the gelatine evenly. Pour the mixture into a 2 litre (3½ pint) mould and chill it until it is firm — at least 4 hours.

Shortly before serving the salad, run the tip of a knife round the inside of the mould to loosen the sides. Briefly dip the bottom of the mould in hot water. Invert a plate on top of the mould, then turn both over together; if necessary, rap the bottom of the mould to free the salad. Lift away the mould and garnish the salad with the lettuce. Serve the salad immediately.

Broccoli Salad with Oven-Roasted Mushrooms

Serves 8 as a first course or side dish
Working (and total) time: about 1 hour and 15 minutes

Calories **105**
Protein **6g**
Cholesterol **0mg**
Total fat **4g**
Saturated fat **0g**
Sodium **150mg**

1 kg	mushrooms, wiped clean, stems trimmed	2 lb
4	large shallots, thinly sliced lengthwise	4
6 tbsp	fresh lemon juice	6 tbsp
2½ tbsp	fresh thyme, or 2 tsp dried thyme	2½ tbsp
¼ tsp	salt	¼ tsp
	freshly ground black pepper	
1 tbsp	safflower oil	1 tbsp
1.25 kg	broccoli, stemmed and cut into florets	2½ lb
1	red or green-leaf lettuce, washed and dried	1
Mustard dressing		
2 tbsp	grainy mustard	2 tbsp
3 tbsp	balsamic vinegar, or 2½ tbsp red wine vinegar mixed with 1 tsp honey	3 tbsp
1 tbsp	chopped parsley	1 tbsp
2 tsp	chopped fresh oregano, or ½ tsp dried oregano	2 tsp
	freshly ground black pepper	
1 tbsp	safflower oil	1 tbsp

Preheat the oven to 230°C (450°F or Mark 8). Put the mushrooms in a large baking dish. Add the shallots, lemon juice, thyme, salt, some pepper and the tablespoon of oil; toss the mixture to coat the mushrooms. Spread the mushrooms in a single layer, then roast them until they are tender and most of the liquid has evaporated — 20 to 25 minutes. Remove the mushrooms from the oven and keep the dish warm.

While the mushrooms are cooking, make the dressing. Combine the mustard, vinegar, parsley, oregano and some pepper in a small bowl. Whisking vigorously, pour in the tablespoon of oil in a thin, steady stream. Continue whisking until the dressing is well combined; set the dressing aside.

Pour enough water into a saucepan to fill it about 2.5 cm (1 inch) deep. Set a vegetable steamer in the pan and bring the water to the boil. Put the broccoli florets into the steamer, cover the pan, and steam the broccoli until it is tender but still crisp — about 4 minutes. Add the broccoli to the dish with the mushrooms. Pour the dressing over the vegetables and toss the salad well. Arrange the salad on a bed of the lettuce leaves; it may be served warm or chilled.

Mango and Grape Salad with Cardamom-Yogurt Dressing

THIS RECIPE CALLS FOR DRIED SKIMMED MILK, WHICH
SERVES TO THICKEN THE DRESSING.

Serves 8 as a first course or side dish
Working (and total) time: about 50 minutes

Calories **110**
Protein **4g**
Cholesterol **2mg**
Total fat **1g**
Saturated fat **0g**
Sodium **30mg**

4	cardamom pods, or ¼ tsp ground cardamom	4
1 tsp	finely grated fresh ginger root	1 tsp
¼ litre	plain low-fat yogurt	8 fl oz
2 tbsp	fresh orange juice	2 tbsp
1 tbsp	honey	1 tbsp
2 tbsp	dried skimmed milk	2 tbsp
1	cos lettuce, washed and dried	1
3	firm mangoes, peeled and cut into 1 cm (½ inch) cubes	3
350 g	seedless red or green grapes, or a mixture of both, halved	12 oz
1 tbsp	coarsely chopped unsalted pistachio nuts	1 tbsp

Remove the cardamom seeds from their pods and grind them with a mortar and pestle. Place the ground spice in a bowl and add the ginger, yogurt, orange juice, honey and dried milk. Whisk the ingredients together. Let the dressing stand at room temperature for at least 20 minutes to thicken it and to allow the different flavours to meld.

To assemble the salad, arrange the lettuce leaves on individual plates and spoon the mango and grapes on to the lettuce. Pour the dressing over each salad and sprinkle the chopped pistachios on top. Serve at once.

Midsummer Melon Salad with Almond Oil

Serves 6 as a first course or side dish
Working time: about 30 minutes
Total time: about 1 hour and 30 minutes (includes chilling)

Calories **120**
Protein **2g**
Cholesterol **0mg**
Total fat **3g**
Saturated fat **0g**
Sodium **70mg**

1	large Charentais melon, seeded, the flesh cut into 4 cm (1½ inch) long pieces	1
½	Gallia or Ogen melon, seeded, the flesh cut into 4 cm (1½ inch) long pieces	½
½	honeydew melon, seeded, the flesh cut into 4 cm (1½ inch) long pieces	½
1 tbsp	coarsely chopped fresh ginger root	1 tbsp
⅛ tsp	salt	⅛ tsp
	freshly ground black pepper	
4 tbsp	rice vinegar	4 tbsp
1 tbsp	almond or walnut oil	1 tbsp

Combine all the melon pieces in a bowl.

Using a mortar and pestle, crush the chopped fresh ginger with the salt and a generous grinding of pepper. Pour in the rice vinegar and continue crushing to extract as much juice from the ginger as possible. Working over the bowl containing the melon, strain the ginger-vinegar mixture through several layers of muslin; twist the corners of the muslin in your hands and squeeze hard so as to extract the last few drops of liquid from the ginger.

Dribble the almond or walnut oil over the melon pieces and gently toss them to distribute the dressing. Serve the salad well chilled.

Savoury Fruit Salad in Red Wine Jelly

Serves 12 as a side dish
Working time: about 30 minutes
Total time: about 4 hours and 30 minutes
(includes chilling)

Calories **110**
Protein **2g**
Cholesterol **0mg**
Total fat **0g**
Saturated fat **0g**
Sodium **5mg**

¾ litre	red wine	1¼ pints
4 tbsp	sugar	4 tbsp
1 tbsp	fresh lemon or lime juice	1 tbsp
10	black peppercorns	10
1	cinnamon stick, broken into pieces	1
1½ tbsp	powdered gelatine, softened in 2 tbsp cold water	1½ tbsp
2	apricots or 1 peach, stoned and cut into 1 cm (½ inch) pieces	2
1	firm yellow apple, quartered, cored and cut into 1 cm (½ inch) pieces	1
2	red plums, stoned and cut into 1 cm (½ inch) pieces	2
160 g	seedless green grapes, halved	5½ oz
160 g	sweet cherries, halved and stoned	5½ oz
300 g	strawberries, stemmed and quartered, any very large quarters cut in half	10 oz
¼ tsp	ground cinnamon	¼ tsp
⅛ tsp	ground cloves	⅛ tsp
	freshly ground black pepper	

To prepare the wine jelly, first pour the wine into a large, non-reactive saucepan; add the sugar, lemon or lime juice, peppercorns and cinnamon stick. Bring the liquid to the boil, then lower the heat to medium and simmer the mixture until it is reduced by half — about 15 minutes. Strain the liquid through a fine sieve into a large bowl. Add the gelatine to the liquid and stir until the gelatine dissolves. Put the bowl into the refrigerator.

When the wine jelly has cooled and become syrupy, stir in the fruit, ground cinnamon, cloves and a generous grinding of pepper. Pour the salad into a 2 litre (3½ pint) mould and chill it until it is firm — about 4 hours.

To unmould the salad, run the tip of a knife around the inside of the mould to loosen the sides. Briefly dip the bottom of the mould into hot water. Invert a plate on top of the mould, then turn both over together; if necessary, rap the bottom of the mould to free the salad. Lift away the mould and serve the salad at once.

EDITOR'S NOTE: *This salad deliciously complements roast lamb, pork or beef, or grilled chicken breasts.*

Fresh Fruit Salad with Cranberry Dressing

Serves 8 as a side dish
Working time: about 15 minutes
Total time: about 25 minutes

Calories **105**
Protein **1g**
Cholesterol **0mg**
Total fat **4g**
Saturated fat **0g**
Sodium **40mg**

45 g	fresh cranberries, or frozen cranberries, thawed	1½ oz
4 tbsp	white vinegar	4 tbsp
1 tbsp	honey	1 tbsp
½ tbsp	finely chopped shallot	½ tbsp
⅛ tsp	salt	⅛ tsp
2 tbsp	safflower oil	2 tbsp
4	tart red apples, cored and cut into cubes	4
325 g	seedless green grapes, halved	11 oz
1	lemon, juice only	1
1	large round lettuce, washed and dried	1

Put the cranberries, vinegar and honey in a small saucepan and bring the mixture to the boil. Reduce the heat to medium low and simmer the mixture until the cranberries are quite soft and the juice has thickened — about 5 minutes. Purée the mixture in a food processor or blender, then strain it through a fine sieve. Set the cranberry purée aside and allow it to cool to room temperature.

Whisk the shallot, salt and oil into the cooled purée. Toss the apples and grapes with the lemon juice. Arrange the lettuce leaves on eight individual plates and spoon the fruit on to the leaves. Ladle the purée evenly over the salad.

2 An array of staples — pinto beans, black beans, chick-peas, lentils, red lentils, black-eyed peas, rice and pasta — awaits transformation into hearty salads.

A New Life for Old Stand-Bys

Such is the versatility of salad that it need not always be made of fresh greens or fruit to find an important place in a meal. Lentils, chick-peas and dried beans, white and brown rice, cracked wheat and barley, wild rice, and pasta — all these and more are the foundation for the 28 appetizing and highly nutritious salads that make up this section.

They have in common their chameleon-like ability to adapt — a quality that serves them well in salads, where they can take on the tastes and aromas of the ingredients with which they are combined.

Among other contributions grains and dried beans make to a salad is texture, whether chewy in the case of wild rice, or pleasantly mealy in the case of beans. To ensure that they preserve their texture, all require careful cooking. A processed grain such as burghul (wheat that has previously been steamed, cracked and dried) has only to be soaked in water for a relatively brief period to make it edible. Whole grains — barley, wheat berries, millet and the like — demand longer cooking. Brown rice, which has a tough outer coating, takes about twice as long to cook as white rice — 35 minutes or more. Dried beans need soaking to soften them — either overnight, or by bringing them to a quick boil and letting them stand for 1 hour — before simmering them in a change of water for 1 to 2 hours. Pasta should be cooked until it is *al dente*, drained and rinsed in cold running water to prevent it from sticking together.

Salads made of grains, dried beans and pasta will obviously be quite a bit more filling than those concocted of greens, and thus some may serve as main courses. Not the least of their attractions is that they can all be prepared in advance — and will often be better when they are, since their flavours then have a chance to develop and mellow.

Brown Rice and Mango Salad

Serves 8 as a side dish
Working time: about 20 minutes
Total time: about 1 hour and 30 minutes

Calories **140**
Protein **2g**
Cholesterol **0mg**
Total fat **4g**
Saturated fat **0g**
Sodium **70mg**

185 g	brown rice	6½ oz
4 tbsp	red wine vinegar	4 tbsp
¼ tsp	salt	¼ tsp
2 tbsp	safflower oil	2 tbsp
1	sweet green pepper, seeded and deribbed	1
1	small shallot, finely chopped	1
⅛ tsp	ground cardamom	⅛ tsp
	mace	
	cayenne pepper	
1	ripe mango, peeled and diced	1

Bring 1.5 litres (2½ pints) of water to the boil in a large saucepan. Stir in the rice, reduce the heat and simmer the rice, uncovered, until it is tender — about 35 minutes. Drain the rice and put it in a serving bowl. Stir in the vinegar and salt, and allow the mixture to cool to room temperature — about 30 minutes.

When the rice is cool, stir in the oil, pepper, shallot, cardamom and a pinch each of mace and cayenne pepper. Add the mango pieces and stir them in gently so that they retain their shape. Cover the salad; to allow the flavours to meld, let the salad stand, unrefrigerated, for about 30 minutes before serving it.

Buckwheat Groats with Wild Mushrooms and Peas

Serves 6 as a side dish
Working (and total) time: about 45 minutes

Calories **110**
Protein **4g**
Cholesterol **0mg**
Total fat **3g**
Saturated fat **0g**
Sodium **90mg**

7 g	dried wild mushrooms	¼ oz
750 g	fresh peas, shelled, or 250 g (8 oz) frozen peas, thawed	1½ lb
200 g	buckwheat groats (kasha)	7 oz
250 g	fresh mushrooms, wiped clean, stems trimmed	8 oz
4 tbsp	fresh lemon juice	4 tbsp
1 tbsp	balsamic vinegar, or ¾ tbsp red wine vinegar mixed with ¼ tsp honey	1 tbsp
1	small shallot, finely chopped	1
¼ tsp	salt	¼ tsp
	freshly ground black pepper	
1 tbsp	safflower oil	1 tbsp

Soak the dried mushrooms in ¼ litre (8 fl oz) of very hot water for 20 minutes, then drain them, reserving their soaking liquid. Chop the mushrooms and set them aside.

If you are using fresh peas, boil them until they are tender — 5 to 7 minutes. (Frozen peas do not require boiling but can be blanched briefly.) Drain the peas and set them aside.

While the mushrooms are soaking, add the buckwheat groats to ½ litre (16 fl oz) of boiling water and cook, stirring frequently, until tender — about 5 minutes. Drain them, rinse well, and drain again. Transfer them to a large bowl.

Slice the fresh mushrooms and put them into a small bowl with the lemon juice; the juice will prevent them from discolouring. Toss the mushrooms well and set the bowl aside.

To prepare the dressing, strain the reserved soaking liquid through a muslin-lined sieve into a small saucepan. Cook the liquid over medium-high heat until only about 2 tablespoons remain — approximately 5 minutes. Pour the liquid into a small bowl; add the lemon juice from the bowl containing the fresh mushrooms, then add the vinegar, shallot, salt and some pepper. Stir the ingredients together. Whisking vigorously, pour in the oil in a thin, steady stream. Continue whisking until the dressing is well combined. Set the dressing aside.

Add the peas, the dried and fresh mushrooms, and the dressing to the buckwheat groats. Combine the ingredients well and serve the salad at once.

Millet Tabbouleh

TABBOULEH, A MIDDLE EASTERN SALAD, IS TRADITIONALLY
MADE WITH BURGHUL. HERE MILLET PROVIDES A NEW TOUCH.

Serves 6 as a side dish
Working time: about 15 minutes
Total time: about 1 hour (includes chilling)

Calories **160**
Protein **4g**
Cholesterol **0mg**
Total fat **4g**
Saturated fat **0g**
Sodium **80mg**

175 g	millet	6 oz
⅛ tsp	salt	⅛ tsp
	freshly ground black pepper	
6 tbsp	raisins	6 tbsp
100 g	stemmed parsley sprigs	3½ oz
1	shallot, finely chopped	1
2 tbsp	finely chopped fresh coriander	2 tbsp
2 tbsp	fresh lemon juice	2 tbsp
2 tsp	honey	2 tsp
2 tsp	Dijon mustard	2 tsp
1 tbsp	safflower oil	1 tbsp
1	large round lettuce, washed and dried	1

Pour ½ litre (16 fl oz) of water into a saucepan and bring it to a simmer over medium heat. Stir in the millet, salt and a generous grinding of pepper. Cover the pan and cook the millet until the water level drops just below the surface of the millet — 10 to 15 minutes. Stir in the raisins and reduce the heat to low; continue cooking the millet, covered, until all the water has been absorbed — about 7 minutes more.

Transfer the contents of the pan to a large bowl. Immediately stir in the parsley sprigs; the hot millet will cook them slightly. Loosely cover the bowl with plastic film and allow the millet to cool.

Meanwhile, combine the shallot, coriander, lemon juice, honey and mustard in a small bowl. Whisk in the oil. When the millet has cooled to room temperature, pour the dressing over it and toss the salad well. Serve chilled with the lettuce.

Polenta Salad with Ham

Serves 6 as a first course or side dish
Working time: about 40 minutes
Total time: about 50 minutes

Calories **140**
Protein **4g**
Cholesterol **5mg**
Total fat **4g**
Saturated fat **1g**
Sodium **220mg**

¼ tsp	salt	¼ tsp
1 tsp	dried oregano, or 1 tbsp chopped fresh oregano	1 tsp
125 g	cornmeal	4 oz
1 tbsp	virgin olive oil	1 tbsp
3	spring onions, trimmed and sliced, white parts kept separate from green	3
500 g	ripe tomatoes, skinned, seeded, chopped	1 lb
4 tbsp	red wine vinegar	4 tbsp
	freshly ground black pepper	
60 g	cooked ham, diced	2 oz

Bring 55 cl (18 fl oz) of water to the boil in a large saucepan with ⅛ teaspoon of the salt and half of the oregano. Sprinkle in the cornmeal, stirring continu-

ously with a wooden spoon. Reduce the heat to medium and cook the polenta, stirring constantly, until all the liquid has been absorbed and the polenta is quite stiff — 10 to 15 minutes. Spoon the polenta on to a large, lightly oiled plate and spread it out to a uniform thickness of about 1 cm (½ inch). Refrigerate the polenta uncovered while you prepare the dressing. Preheat the oven to 180°C (350°F or Mark 4).

Heat the oil in a heavy frying pan over medium heat. Add the white spring onion parts and the remaining oregano, and cook them for 1 minute. Stir in the tomatoes, vinegar, the remaining salt and some pepper. Cook the mixture, stirring occasionally, for 15 minutes. Transfer the contents of the pan to a blender or food processor, and purée the mixture until a smooth dressing results. Pour the dressing into a large bowl and chill it while you finish the salad.

Cut the polenta into strips about 1 cm (½ inch) wide and 4 cm (1½ inches) long. Transfer the strips to a lightly oiled baking sheet and bake them for 10 minutes to dry them out, turning them occasionally with a metal spatula. Immediately transfer the strips to the bowl with the dressing. Add the green spring onion parts, the ham and a generous grinding of pepper. Toss the salad well and serve it without delay.

Apricots and Water Chestnuts in Wild Rice

Serves 8 as a side dish
Working time: about 30 minutes
Total time: about 1 hour

Calories **130**
Protein **4g**
Cholesterol **0mg**
Total fat **0g**
Saturated fat **0g**
Sodium **75mg**

160 g	wild rice	5½ oz
125 g	dried apricots, cut into 1 cm (½ inch) pieces	4 oz
175 g	fresh water chestnuts, peeled and quartered, or 250 g (8 oz) canned whole peeled water chestnuts, drained, rinsed and quartered	6 oz
2 tbsp	chopped parsley	2 tbsp
	Spicy lemon dressing	
2 tbsp	fresh lemon juice	2 tbsp
1 tbsp	red wine vinegar	1 tbsp
⅛ tsp	ground ginger	⅛ tsp
⅛ tsp	cinnamon	⅛ tsp
	ground cloves	
¼ tsp	salt	¼ tsp
	freshly ground black pepper	

Bring 1.5 litres (2½ pints) of water to the boil in a saucepan. Stir in the wild rice, reduce the heat, and simmer the rice, uncovered, until it is tender but still chewy — approximately 45 minutes.

While the rice cooks, prepare the apricots and dressing: put the apricots into a small bowl and pour in enough hot water to cover them by about 2.5 cm (1 inch). Soak the apricots for 20 minutes to soften them. Drain the apricots, reserving 4 tablespoons of their soaking liquid, and set them aside.

Pour the reserved apricot-soaking liquid into a small bowl. Add the lemon juice, vinegar, ginger, cinnamon, a pinch of cloves, the salt and some pepper; whisk the mixture vigorously until it is thoroughly combined.

When the rice finishes cooking, drain and rinse it, and transfer it to a serving bowl. Pour the dressing over the rice, then add the apricots, water chestnuts and the parsley; toss the ingredients well and serve the salad at room temperature.

Saffron Rice Salad with Peppers and Chick-Peas

Serves 12 as a side dish
Working time: about 30 minutes
Total time: about 2 hours and 45 minutes

Calories **180**
Protein **5g**
Cholesterol **0mg**
Total fat **7g**
Saturated fat **1g**
Sodium **145mg**

135 g	dried chick-peas, picked over	4½ oz
¼ tsp	salt	¼ tsp
275 g	long-grain rice	9 oz
60 cl	unsalted chicken stock or water	1 pint
½ tsp	saffron threads, soaked for 10 minutes in very hot water	½ tsp
1	strip lemon rind	1
500 g	fresh peas, shelled, or 150 g (5 oz) frozen peas, thawed	1 lb
30 g	whole unskinned almonds	1 oz
1	sweet red pepper, seeded, deribbed and cut into thin slices	1
1	sweet green pepper, seeded, deribbed and cut into thin slices	1
2	ripe tomatoes, seeded and chopped	2
6	oil-cured black olives, thinly sliced	6
6 tbsp	vinaigrette (recipe, page 13)	6 tbsp

Rinse the chick-peas under cold running water. Put the chick-peas in a large, heavy pan and pour in enough cold water to cover them by about 5 cm (2 inches). Discard any chick-peas that float to the surface. Cover the pan, leaving the lid ajar, and bring the water to the boil; cook for 2 minutes. Turn off the heat, cover the pan, and soak the peas for at least 1 hour. (Alternatively, soak the chick-peas overnight in cold water.)

When the chick-peas finish soaking, drain them well in a colander. Return them to the pan and pour in enough water to cover them by about 5 cm (2 inches). Bring the liquid to a simmer; cook the chick-peas over medium-low heat until they are soft — about 45 minutes. Stir in the salt and continue cooking the chick-peas until they are quite tender — 10 to 15 minutes more. (If the chick-peas appear to be drying out at any point, pour in more water.)

About 20 minutes before the chick-peas finish cooking, start the rice: bring the stock or water to the boil in a saucepan, then add the rice, the saffron and its soaking liquid, and the lemon rind. Stir the rice to distribute the saffron and return the liquid to the boil. Cover the pan and cook the rice over medium-low heat until it is tender and has absorbed all the liquid — about 20 minutes. Discard the lemon rind. ▶

While the rice is cooking, boil the fresh peas until they are tender — 5 to 7 minutes. (Frozen peas do not require boiling but can be blanched briefly.) Drain the peas and set them aside. Heat the almonds in a small, heavy frying pan over medium heat, stirring frequently until they are lightly toasted — about 5 minutes.

Drain the chick-peas well and transfer them to a large bowl. Add the rice, peas, toasted almonds, red and green peppers, tomatoes and olives. Pour the prepared vinaigrette over the salad and toss the ingredients well to coat them. Transfer the salad to a serving dish. Serve at room temperature or barely chilled.

Calories **280**
Protein **6g**
Cholesterol **0mg**
Total fat **5g**
Saturated fat **1g**
Sodium **125mg**

Wheat Berry and Orange Salad

Serves 6 as a first course or side dish
Working time: about 45 minutes
Total time: about 2 hours

190 g	wheat berries	6½ oz
¼ tsp	salt	¼ tsp
6	large sweet oranges (about 250 g/8 oz each)	6
75 g	raisins	2½ oz
2 tsp	sherry vinegar or red wine vinegar	2 tsp
1 tbsp	grainy mustard	1 tbsp
2 tbsp	virgin olive oil	2 tbsp
	freshly ground black pepper	
1 tsp	grated orange rind	1 tsp
45 g	spring onions, thinly sliced	1½ oz
4 tbsp	thinly sliced mint leaves	4 tbsp
6	mint sprigs for garnish	6

Bring ½ litre (16 fl oz) of water to the boil in a saucepan. Stir in the wheat berries and salt. Reduce the heat to low, cover the pan, and simmer the kernels until they are tender — 1½ to 2 hours. If the wheat berries absorb all the water before they finish cooking, pour in more water, 4 tablespoons at a time, to keep the kernels from burning. Drain the wheat berries and set them aside to cool.

While the wheat berries are cooking, hollow out the oranges as shown. Using your fingers, a knife or a spoon, separate 90 g (3 oz) of the orange flesh from the pulp; coarsely chop the flesh and set it aside. Squeeze the juice from the remaining pulp and reserve 12.5 cl (4 fl oz) of it. (Save the rest of the juice for another use.) Combine the measured juice in a small bowl with the raisins; let the raisins soak for 15 minutes.

To prepare the dressing, transfer 2 tablespoons of the raisin-soaking liquid to a large bowl. Add the vinegar and mustard. Slowly whisk in the oil, then season the dressing with some pepper.

Add to the bowl the drained wheat berries, chopped orange flesh, orange rind, raisins with their remaining soaking liquid, spring onion and sliced mint. Stir to combine the ingredients, then spoon the mixture into the orange shells. Replace the orange tops and garnish each shell with a sprig of mint before serving.

How to Make an Orange Cup

1 *REMOVING THE TOP. With a boning knife, as here, or a paring knife, slice off the top of an orange about 2.5 cm (1 inch) from the stem end. Reserve the top to use as a cover for the cup; to prevent drying, place the top flesh side down on a plate.*

2 *CUTTING ROUND THE CORE. Holding the orange at an angle, insert the knife tip between the flesh and the peel, and dig deep into the fruit. With a gentle sawing motion, cut round the rim to separate as much of the flesh from the peel as possible.*

3 *EXTRACTING THE FLESH. Hold the orange over a bowl to catch the juice, and insert a sturdy soup spoon into the cut. Dig round the cut with the spoon, while rotating the orange in your other hand. Scoop out the core.*

4 *EMPTYING THE SHELL. Grasping the spoon firmly, dig under the membrane to remove the residual pulp and juice. Scrape the interior thoroughly to bare the white wall.*

Burghul Salad with Raisins and Courgettes

Serves 12 as a side dish
Working time: about 20 minutes
Total time: about 1 hour and 30 minutes
(includes soaking and chilling)

Calories **125**
Protein **4g**
Cholesterol **0mg**
Total fat **1g**
Saturated fat **0g**
Sodium **5mg**

325 g	burghul	11 oz
2	courgettes, each cut crosswise into 5 mm (¼ inch) slices, each slice cut into eight wedges	2
5	spring onions, trimmed and sliced	5
12.5 cl	red wine vinegar	4 fl oz
1	sweet yellow pepper, seeded, deribbed and cut into 1 cm (½ inch) squares	1
4 tbsp	raisins	4 tbsp
⅛ tsp	cayenne pepper	⅛ tsp
⅛ tsp	ground cardamom	⅛ tsp
⅛ tsp	ground coriander	⅛ tsp
	ground cloves	
	ground ginger	
	ground mace	

Put the burghul into a heatproof bowl and pour ¾ litre (1¼ pints) of boiling water over it. Cover the bowl and set it aside for 30 minutes.

At the end of the soaking period, mix in the courgettes, spring onions, vinegar, yellow pepper, raisins, cayenne pepper, cardamom, coriander, and a pinch each of cloves, ginger and mace. Let the salad stand for at least 30 minutes before serving it either chilled or at room temperature.

Chick-Pea Purée on Cos Lettuce Leaves

Serves 8 as a first course or side dish
Working time: about 45 minutes
Total time: about 3 hours (includes soaking)

Calories **70**
Protein **5g**
Cholesterol **2mg**
Total fat **3g**
Saturated fat **0g**
Sodium **60mg**

200 g	chick-peas, picked over	7 oz
1	garlic clove, quartered	1
4 tbsp	celery leaves	4 tbsp
4 tbsp	freshly grated Parmesan cheese	4 tbsp
2 tbsp	pine-nuts	2 tbsp
4 tbsp	fresh lemon juice	4 tbsp
⅛ tsp	white pepper	⅛ tsp
2	cos lettuces, washed and dried	2
1	small ripe tomato, chopped	1
2 tbsp	chopped red onion	2 tbsp
2 tbsp	chopped sweet green pepper (optional)	2 tbsp

Rinse the chick-peas under cold running water, then transfer them to a large pan and pour in enough water to cover them by about 5 cm (2 inches). Discard any chick-peas that float to the surface. Cover the pan, leaving the lid ajar, and bring the liquid to the boil; cook the peas for 2 minutes. Turn off the heat, cover the pan, and soak the peas for at least 1 hour. (Alternatively, soak the peas overnight in cold water.)

At the end of the soaking period, drain the chick-peas and return them to the pan with ¾ litre (1¼ pints) of water. Bring the liquid to a strong simmer, then reduce the heat to medium low, and cook the peas, covered, until they are quite tender — about 1¼ hours. (If the peas appear to be drying out at any point, pour in more water, ¼ litre/8 fl oz at a time.)

Drain the chick-peas, catching their cooking liquid in a bowl. Set the bowl aside. Press the chick-peas through a sieve, then put them in a blender or food processor with the garlic, celery leaves, Parmesan cheese, pine-nuts, 3 tablespoons of the lemon juice and the white pepper. With the motor running, pour in ¼ litre (8 fl oz) of the reserved cooking liquid in a slow, thin stream — a smooth paste should result. If need be, incorporate as much as 12.5 cl (4 fl oz) of additional cooking liquid. (Unsalted chicken stock or water may be used to augment the cooking liquid.)

Remove the outer lettuce leaves and reserve them for another use. Spread about 1 tablespoon of the chick-pea purée over the stem end of each inner leaf. Mound the remaining purée in the middle of a serving plate and arrange the leaves around it. Chill the salad for at least 20 minutes. Just before serving, garnish the salad with the tomato, the onion and the green pepper if you are using it; dribble the remaining lemon juice over the top of the purée.

Black Bean, Rice and Pepper Salad

Serves 4 as a main course
Working time: about 20 minutes
Total time: about 11 hours (includes soaking and chilling)

Calories **635**
Protein **21g**
Cholesterol **2mg**
Total fat **10g**
Saturated fat **1g**
Sodium **385mg**

185 g	black beans, picked over, soaked for 8 hours (or overnight) and drained	6½ oz
1	small onion, coarsely chopped	1
1	garlic clove	1
2 tsp	fresh thyme, or ½ tsp dried thyme leaves	2 tsp
1	bay leaf	1
½ tsp	salt	½ tsp
1 litre	unsalted chicken stock	1¾ pints
370 g	long-grain rice	13 oz
2	shallots, finely chopped	2
1	sweet red pepper, seeded, deribbed and sliced into short, thin strips	1
1	sweet green pepper, seeded, deribbed and sliced into short, thin strips	1
1	fresh hot green chili pepper, seeded and finely chopped (caution, page 17)	1
3	spring onions, trimmed and thinly sliced	3
2 tbsp	chopped fresh coriander or parsley	2 tbsp
Chili dressing		
1 tsp	Dijon mustard	1 tsp
1 tbsp	sherry vinegar or white wine vinegar	1 tbsp
1 tbsp	unsalted chicken stock	1 tbsp
2 tbsp	virgin olive oil	2 tbsp
½ tsp	chili powder	½ tsp
4	drops Tabasco sauce	4
1	garlic clove, finely chopped	1
	freshly ground black pepper	

Put the beans into a large, heavy-bottomed saucepan, and pour in enough cold water to cover them by about 7.5 cm (3 inches). Bring the water to the boil. Boil the beans for 10 minutes, then drain.

Return the beans to the pan, add enough water to cover them by 7.5 cm (3 inches) and bring to the boil. Add the onion, garlic, thyme and bay leaf to the beans, tightly cover the pan and simmer the beans, occasionally skimming foam from the surface of the liquid, until they are soft — about 50 minutes. Stir in the salt and continue cooking the beans until they are quite tender — 30 minutes to 1 hour more. If the beans appear to be drying out at any point, pour in more water.

Transfer the cooked beans to a colander. Remove the garlic clove and bay leaf, then rinse the beans and drain them well.

Bring the stock to the boil in a small saucepan. Add the rice and shallots, and lower the heat to maintain a simmer. Cook the rice, covered, until it is tender and the liquid is absorbed — about 20 minutes.

While the rice is cooking, prepare the dressing. Combine the mustard, vinegar and the tablespoon of stock in a small bowl. Whisk in the oil, then the chili powder, Tabasco sauce, garlic and some pepper.

Transfer the hot rice to a large bowl. Add the peppers, spring onions and beans. Pour the dressing over the salad, toss well, and chill the salad for at least 1 hour. Sprinkle the salad with the fresh coriander or parsley just before serving.

EDITOR'S NOTE: *Instead of soaking the beans overnight, they can be put in a pan with enough cold water to cover by 7.5 cm (3 inches), boiled for 2 minutes, then left to soak (off the heat and covered) for at least 1 hour, and drained.*

Red Lentils with White Rice and Pearl Onions

Serves 6 as a side dish
Working time: about 15 minutes
Total time: about 30 minutes

Calories **200**
Protein **8g**
Cholesterol **0mg**
Total fat **3g**
Saturated fat **0g**
Sodium **20mg**

190 g	red lentils, picked over	6½ oz
90 g	long-grain rice	3 oz
2 tbsp	sugar	2 tbsp
4 tbsp	raspberry vinegar	4 tbsp
6 tbsp	unsalted chicken stock	6 tbsp
175 g	pearl onions, blanched for 2 minutes in boiling water and peeled	6 oz
1 tsp	Dijon mustard	1 tsp
	freshly ground black pepper	
1 tbsp	safflower oil	1 tbsp

Bring the lentils and ¾ litre (1¼ pints) of water to the boil in a small saucepan over medium-high heat. Reduce the heat and simmer the lentils until they are tender — 15 to 20 minutes. Avoid overcooking or the lentils will lose much of their colour. Drain the lentils and put them into a large bowl.

Start cooking the rice while the lentils are simmering. Bring the rice and ¼ litre (8 fl oz) of water to the boil in a small saucepan over medium-high heat. Reduce the heat, cover the saucepan, and simmer the rice until the liquid has been absorbed and the rice is tender — about 20 minutes. Add the rice to the lentils.

While the rice is cooking, sprinkle the sugar into a sauté pan and set it over medium heat. Cook the sugar until it liquefies and starts to caramelize. Pour in 3 tablespoons of the vinegar and 4 tablespoons of the chicken stock. As the liquid comes to a simmer, stir it to incorporate the caramelized sugar, then add the pearl onions. Cook the onions, stirring from time to time, until they are glazed and nearly all the liquid in the pan has evaporated. Add the glazed onions to the lentils and rice in the bowl.

To prepare the dressing, combine the remaining raspberry vinegar and chicken stock, the mustard and some pepper in a small bowl. Whisk in the oil, then pour the vinaigrette over the lentil and rice mixture, and toss well. This salad is best served cold.

Aubergine, Cucumber and White Bean Salad

Serves 12 as a side dish
Working time: about 30 minutes
Total time: about 3 hours (includes soaking and chilling)

Calories **120**
Protein **7g**
Cholesterol **0mg**
Total fat **1g**
Saturated fat **0g**
Sodium **95mg**

500 g	dried haricot beans, picked over	1 lb
350 g	aubergine, cut into 1 cm (½ inch) cubes	12 oz
1	onion, chopped	1
½ tsp	caster sugar	½ tsp
4 tbsp	raspberry vinegar or red wine vinegar	4 tbsp
1 tsp	chopped fresh sage, or ¼ tsp dried sage, crushed	1 tsp
1	garlic clove, finely chopped	1
½ tsp	salt	½ tsp
	freshly ground black pepper	
1	cucumber, cut into 1 cm (½ inch) cubes	1

Rinse the beans under cold running water, then put them into a large, heavy pan, and pour in enough cold water to cover them by about 7.5 cm (3 inches). Discard any beans that float to the surface. Cover the pan, leaving the lid ajar, and slowly bring the liquid to the boil. Boil the beans for 2 minutes, then turn off the heat, and soak the beans, covered, for at least 1 hour. (Alternatively, soak the beans overnight in cold water.)

Preheat the oven to 240°C (475°F or Mark 9).

If the beans have absorbed all of their soaking liquid, pour in enough water to cover them again by about 7.5 cm (3 inches). Bring the liquid to the boil, reduce the heat to maintain a strong simmer, and cook the beans until they are tender — about 1 hour.

While the beans are cooking, put the aubergine cubes into a lightly oiled baking dish and bake them until they are a golden-brown — about 20 minutes. Meanwhile, combine the onion with the sugar and 2 tablespoons of the vinegar; set the mixture aside. When the aubergine cubes are browned, transfer them to a bowl; toss the cubes with the remaining 2 tablespoons of vinegar and set the bowl aside until the beans finish cooking.

Drain the cooked beans and rinse them under cold running water. Combine them with the marinated aubergine and onion. Add the sage, garlic, salt, some pepper and the cucumber, and mix well. Serve the salad at room temperature or chill it for at least 30 minutes before serving.

Red and White Bean Salad

KIDNEY BEANS CONTAIN TOXINS CALLED LECTINS. TO DESTROY THE
LECTINS, THE BEANS SHOULD BE COOKED AT A LIGHT BOIL FOR
10 MINUTES AND THE WATER DISCARDED.

Serves 8 as a first course or side dish
Working time: about 25 minutes
Total time: about 9 hours and 20 minutes
(includes soaking)

Calories **200**
Protein **11g**
Cholesterol **0mg**
Total fat **3g**
Saturated fat **0g**
Sodium **95mg**

250 g	red kidney beans, soaked for 8 hours (or overnight) and drained	8 oz
250 g	dried haricot or cannellini beans, soaked for 8 hours (or overnight) and drained	8 oz
1	small celeriac	1
1	small onion, thinly sliced	1
2 tsp	finely chopped fresh ginger root	2 tsp
4 tbsp	red wine vinegar	4 tbsp
¼ tsp	salt	¼ tsp
	freshly ground black pepper	
1 tbsp	chopped fresh coriander	1 tbsp
1	large, ripe tomato, chopped	1
1½ tbsp	safflower oil	1½ tbsp

Put the kidney beans and haricot beans into two separate large saucepans with enough cold water to cover by about 7.5 cm (3 inches). Bring to the boil. Boil the kidney beans for 10 minutes, then turn down the heat to simmer. When the haricot beans come to the boil, turn the heat down to simmer. Simmer both beans until tender — 50 to 60 minutes cooking time in all.

Meanwhile, peel the celeriac and cut it into 1 cm (½ inch) cubes. Transfer the cubes to a salad bowl and toss them with the onion, ginger and vinegar. Set aside.

Drain the cooked beans and rinse them under cold water. Drain again and add them to the bowl with the salt, some pepper, the coriander, tomato and oil; mix well, and served chilled or at room temperature.

EDITOR'S NOTE: *Instead of overnight soaking, the beans can be put in a pan with enough cold water to cover by 7.5 cm (3 inches), boiled for 2 minutes, then left to stand (off the heat and covered) for at least 1 hour, and drained.*

Lentil and Mushroom Salad

Serves 6 as a side dish
Working time: about 40 minutes
Total time: about 1 hour and 40 minutes
(includes chilling)

Calories **165**
Protein **8g**
Cholesterol **0mg**
Total fat **5g**
Saturated fat **1g**
Sodium **165mg**

140 g	lentils, picked over	4½ oz
1	small onion, studded with 4 whole cloves	1
1	bay leaf	1
2 tsp	fresh thyme, or ½ tsp dried thyme	2 tsp
3	carrots, thinly sliced	3
3	sticks celery, sliced	3
3	spring onions, trimmed and thinly sliced	3
175 g	mushrooms, wiped clean, trimmed and thinly sliced	6 oz
2 tbsp	fresh lemon juice	2 tbsp
3 or 4	cos lettuce leaves, cut into chiffonade (page 51)	3 or 4
2	ripe tomatoes, each cut into 8 wedges	2
1 tbsp	chopped parsley	1 tbsp
Spicy mustard vinaigrette		
1 tbsp	Dijon mustard	1 tbsp
2 tbsp	fresh lemon juice	2 tbsp
2 tsp	Tabasco sauce	2 tsp
2	garlic cloves, finely chopped	2
¼ tsp	salt	¼ tsp
	freshly ground black pepper	
2 tbsp	virgin olive oil	2 tbsp

Rinse the lentils and put them into a saucepan with 1 litre (1¾ pints) of water. Add the onion, bay leaf and thyme, and bring the water to the boil. Reduce the heat to maintain a simmer and cook the lentils until they are tender — about 25 minutes. Drain the lentils, discard the onion and the bay leaf, and transfer the lentils to a large bowl. Add the carrots, celery and

spring onions, and toss the mixture well.

Put the mushrooms and the lemon juice into a saucepan; pour in enough water to just cover the mushrooms, and bring the water to the boil. Cover the pan, reduce the heat, and simmer the mushrooms until they are tender — about 5 minutes. Drain the mushrooms and add them to the bowl containing the other vegetables.

To prepare the vinaigrette, whisk together the mustard, lemon juice, Tabasco sauce, garlic, salt, some pepper and the oil. Pour the vinaigrette over the lentil mixture, toss well, and refrigerate it for at least 1 hour.

To serve the salad, mound the lentil mixture in the centre of a serving plate and arrange the lettuce around the lentil salad. Garnish with the tomato wedges and sprinkle the chopped parsley over all.

Curried Black-Eyed Peas

Serves 6 as a side dish
Working time: about 20 minutes
Total time: about 2 hours and 30 minutes
(includes soaking and chilling)

Calories **105**
Protein **5g**
Cholesterol **0mg**
Total fat **3g**
Saturated fat **0g**
Sodium **100mg**

170 g	black-eyed peas, picked over	6 oz
¼ tsp	salt	¼ tsp
12.5 cl	unsalted chicken stock	4 fl oz
2	bunches spring onions, trimmed and cut into 2.5 cm (1 inch) lengths	2
1½ tbsp	fresh lemon juice	1½ tbsp
1 tbsp	red wine vinegar or white wine vinegar	1 tbsp
½ tbsp	honey	½ tbsp
1¼ tsp	curry powder	1¼ tsp
	freshly ground black pepper	
1 tbsp	virgin olive oil	1 tbsp
½	sweet red pepper, seeded, deribbed and cut into bâtonnets	½

Rinse the black-eyed peas under cold running water, then put them into a large saucepan, and pour in enough cold water to cover them by about 7.5 cm (3 inches). Discard any peas that float to the surface. Bring the water to the boil and cook the peas for 2 minutes. Turn off the heat, partially cover the pan, and soak the peas for at least 1 hour. (Alternatively, soak the peas overnight in cold water.)

Bring the peas to a simmer over medium-low heat and tightly cover the pan. Cook the peas, occasionally skimming any foam from the surface of the liquid, until they begin to soften — about 45 minutes. Stir in the salt and continue cooking the peas until they are quite tender — about 15 minutes more. If the peas appear to be drying out at any point, pour in more water.

While the peas are cooking, heat the stock in a large frying pan over medium heat. Add the spring onions and partially cover the pan. Cook the spring onions, stirring often, until almost all the liquid has evaporated — 8 to 10 minutes. Transfer the contents of the pan to a bowl.

In a smaller bowl, combine the lemon juice, vinegar, honey, curry powder and some pepper. Whisk in the oil and set the dressing aside.

Transfer the cooked peas to a colander; rinse and drain them. Add the peas and the red pepper to the spring onions in the bowl. Pour the dressing over all and toss the salad well. Chill the salad for at least 30 minutes before serving.

Lentil Salad
with Sweet Red Peppers

Serves 12 as a side dish
Working time: about 1 hour
Total time: about 3 hours (includes chilling)

Calories **130**
Protein **6g**
Cholesterol **11mg**
Total fat **5g**
Saturated fat **1g**
Sodium **140mg**

275 g	lentils, picked over and rinsed	9 oz
4 tbsp	finely chopped fresh tarragon, or 2 tbsp dried tarragon	4 tbsp
4 tbsp	tarragon vinegar	4 tbsp
3	sweet red peppers	3
4 tbsp	virgin olive oil	4 tbsp
8	large garlic cloves	8
17.5 cl	fresh lemon juice	6 fl oz
4 tbsp	finely sliced chives or spring onions	4 tbsp

3 tbsp	finely chopped fresh chervil (optional)	3 tbsp
¾ tsp	salt	¾ tsp
	freshly ground black pepper	
1	hard-boiled egg	1
1	cucumber	1
2 or 3	small ripe tomatoes, sliced	2 or 3

Put the lentils in a large, heavy saucepan with ¾ litre (1¼ pints) of water. Bring the water to the boil, then reduce the heat to medium and simmer the lentils until they are tender — about 20 minutes.

If you are using dried tarragon, combine it with the vinegar in a small, non-reactive pan set over medium heat. Bring the liquid to a simmer, then remove the pan from the heat and allow the tarragon to steep for at least 10 minutes.

While the lentils are cooking, roast the peppers about 5 cm (2 inches) below a preheated grill, turning them until they are blistered on all sides. Place the peppers in a bowl and cover it with plastic film; the trapped steam will loosen their skins. Peel and seed the peppers, then finely chop them; set the chopped peppers aside.

Drain the lentils and transfer them to a large bowl. Combine the oil and vinegar in a small bowl and pour the liquid over the lentils. Add the chopped peppers and stir the mixture well, then refrigerate it.

Preheat the oven to 240°C (475°F or Mark 9). Place the garlic cloves in a small, ovenproof dish and bake them until they are soft — 7 to 10 minutes. When the cloves are cool enough to handle, peel them and press them through a sieve set over a bowl. Whisk the lemon juice into the garlic purée, then stir the purée into the lentil-pepper mixture. Add the chives or spring onions, the fresh tarragon and chervil if you are using them, the salt and some pepper, stir well to combine all the ingredients. Refrigerate the salad for at least 2 hours before serving it.

At serving time, shell the egg and separate the yolk from the white. Press the yolk through a sieve set over a small bowl. Sieve the egg white the same way. Mound the salad on a serving plate; sprinkle half of the egg white and then half of the yolk over the top. (Alternatively, the whole egg may be used, but doing so will raise the cholesterol level above our guidelines for a side dish.) Cutting the length of the cucumber with a vegetable peeler, pare off alternating strips of skin to achieve a striped effect. Thinly slice the cucumber. Garnish the lentil salad with the sliced cucumber and tomatoes.

EDITOR'S NOTE. *The flavour of this salad will be even better a day later. If you prepare the salad in advance, store in the refrigerator; do not add the garnishes until serving time.*

Chick-Pea Salad with Cucumber and Dill Sauce

Serves 6 as a side dish
Working time: about 25 minutes
Total time: about 2 hours and 30 minutes
(includes soaking)

Calories **80**
Protein **5g**
Cholesterol **3mg**
Total fat **2g**
Saturated fat **1g**
Sodium **115mg**

200 g	chick-peas, picked over	7 oz
2	cucumbers	2
1	large tomato, skinned, seeded and coarsely chopped	1
4 tbsp	finely cut fresh dill	4 tbsp
12.5 cl	plain low-fat yogurt	4 fl oz
2 tbsp	soured cream	2 tbsp
¼ tsp	salt	¼ tsp
	freshly ground black pepper	

Rinse the chick-peas under cold running water, then put them in a large, heavy pan and pour in enough cold water to cover them by about 7.5 cm (3 inches). Discard any that float to the surface. Cover the pan, leaving the lid ajar, and slowly bring the liquid to the boil over medium-low heat. Boil the chick-peas for 2 minutes, then turn off the heat and soak them for at least 1 hour. (Alternatively, soak the peas overnight in cold water.) If they absorb all the liquid, add enough water to cover them again by about 7.5 cm (3 inches). Bring the liquid to the boil, reduce the heat to maintain a strong simmer, and cook the peas until they are tender — about 1 hour. Drain the peas, rinse them under cold running water, and transfer them to a salad bowl.

Cut one cucumber into thin slices and set the slices aside. Peel the remaining cucumber and seed it. Finely chop the flesh and place it on a large square of doubled muslin. Gather the ends and twist them to wring out as much moisture as possible from the cucumber. Discard the juice.

Combine the chopped cucumber, tomato, dill, yogurt, soured cream, salt and some pepper with the chick-peas, and gently toss the mixture. Serve the salad garnished with the reserved cucumber slices.

Couscous Salad with Mange-Tout and Wild Mushrooms

Serves 6 as a first course or side dish
Working time: about 20 minutes
Total time: about 35 minutes

Calories **135**
Protein **5g**
Cholesterol **0mg**
Total fat **4g**
Saturated fat **1g**
Sodium **150mg**

35 cl	unsalted chicken stock	12 fl oz
4 tbsp	chopped shallot	4 tbsp
2½ tbsp	fresh lemon juice	2½ tbsp
	freshly ground black pepper	
175 g	couscous	6 oz
6 tbsp	coarsely chopped fresh coriander	6 tbsp
1½ tbsp	virgin olive oil	1½ tbsp
125 g	fresh ceps, chanterelles or other wild mushrooms, wiped clean and sliced	4 oz
1 tsp	fresh thyme, or ¼ tsp dried thyme	1 tsp
125 g	mange-tout, stems and strings removed, each cut diagonally into 3 pieces	4 oz
¼ tsp	salt	¼ tsp
1 tsp	red wine vinegar	1 tsp
1	oakleaf lettuce or red-leaf lettuce, washed and dried	1

Pour the stock into a large saucepan; add 2 tablespoons of the shallot, 2 tablespoons of the lemon juice and some pepper. Bring the stock to the boil, then stir in the couscous and half of the coriander. Cover the pan tightly and remove it from the heat; let it stand while you complete the salad.

Meanwhile, heat 1 tablespoon of the oil in a large, heavy frying pan over medium-high heat. When the oil is hot, add the mushrooms, thyme and the remaining shallot. Sauté the mushrooms until they begin to brown — about 4 minutes. Stir in the mange-tout, the salt and some pepper. Cook the mixture, stirring frequently, for 2 minutes more. Remove the pan from the heat.

Transfer the couscous to a large bowl and fluff it with a fork. In a small bowl, combine the vinegar, the remaining oil, the remaining lemon juice and the remaining coriander. Dribble this vinaigrette over the couscous and fluff the couscous once again to distribute the dressing evenly. Add the contents of the frying pan to the bowl, using a rubber spatula to scrape out the flavour-rich juices. Toss the salad well and chill it for at least 15 minutes.

To serve, arrange the lettuce on a serving platter and mound the salad on top of the leaves.

Chilled Spinach Spirals with Prawns, Aubergine and Yellow Squash

Serves 6 as a main course
Working time: about 35 minutes
Total time: about 45 minutes

Calories **260**
Protein **16g**
Cholesterol **80mg**
Total fat **6g**
Saturated fat **1g**
Sodium **250mg**

2 tbsp	virgin olive oil	2 tbsp
2½ tbsp	fresh lime juice	2½ tbsp
1	aubergine (about 175 g/6 oz), halved lengthwise, the halves cut crosswise into 1 cm (½ inch) thick slices	1
250 g	spinach pasta spirals or other fancy spinach pasta	8 oz
250 g	ripe tomatoes	8 oz
1	large yellow squash or courgette (about 125 g/4 oz), halved lengthwise, halves cut diagonally into 1 cm (½ inch) thick slices	1
2	shallots, finely chopped	2
350 g	fresh prawns, peeled, and deveined if necessary	12 oz
1 tsp	fresh thyme, or ¼ tsp dried thyme	1 tsp
¼ tsp	salt	¼ tsp
	freshly ground black pepper	
60 g	goat cheese	2 oz
4 tbsp	plain low-fat yogurt	4 tbsp
2 tbsp	milk	2 tbsp

Preheat the grill. Bring 3 litres (5 pints) of water to the boil in a large saucepan.

Meanwhile, mix 1 tablespoon of the oil with 1 tablespoon of the lime juice and brush the mixture over both sides of the aubergine slices. Set the slices on a baking sheet and grill them on one side until lightly browned — 3 to 4 minutes. Turn and grill them on the second side. Let them cool before transferring to a large bowl. Put the bowl into the refrigerator.

Add the spinach pasta to the boiling water with 1½ teaspoons of salt. Start testing the pasta for doneness after 10 minutes and cook it until it is *al dente*. Drain the pasta, rinse it under cold running water, and drain it again. Add the pasta to the bowl with the aubergine.

While the pasta is cooking, cut the tomatoes into strips: place each tomato, stem end down, on a clean work surface. With a small, sharp knife, cut the flesh from the tomato in wide, flat sections; discard the pulpy core and seeds. Slice the sections lengthwise into strips about 5 mm (¼ inch) wide and set them aside.

Heat the remaining oil in a large, heavy frying pan over medium-high heat. When the oil is hot, add the squash and shallots. Cook the vegetables, stirring ▶

frequently, for 1 minute. Add the prawns, thyme, salt, some pepper and the remaining lime juice, and sauté the mixture until the prawns are just cooked through — about 2 minutes. Stir in the tomato strips and cook the mixture for 30 seconds more. Transfer the contents of the frying pan to the bowl with the pasta and aubergine, and toss the mixture well; return the bowl to the refrigerator.

To prepare the dressing, put the cheese, yogurt, milk and a liberal grinding of black pepper into a blender or food processor. Purée the mixture, scraping down the sides at least once. Add the dressing to the salad; toss the salad well and chill it briefly before serving.

Orzo with Pistachio Pesto

Serves 8 as a side dish
Working time: about 15 minutes
Total time: about 35 minutes

Calories **160**
Protein **6g**
Cholesterol **3mg**
Total fat **5g**
Saturated fat **1g**
Sodium **140mg**

250 g	orzo (rice-shaped pasta) or farfallini	8 oz
1	sweet yellow pepper, seeded, deribbed and cut into small dice	1
2 tbsp	white wine vinegar	2 tbsp
Pistachio pesto		
45 g	celery leaves, several leaves reserved for garnish	1½ oz
25 g	pistachio nuts, coarsely chopped	¾ oz
1 tbsp	virgin olive oil	1 tbsp
1	garlic clove, finely chopped	1
12.5 cl	unsalted chicken stock	4 fl oz
30 g	Parmesan cheese, freshly grated	1 oz

Add the pasta with ½ teaspoon of salt to 1 litre (1¾ pints) of boiling water. Start testing the pasta for doneness after 8 minutes and cook it until it is *al dente*.

Meanwhile, combine the yellow pepper and the vinegar in a large bowl. Drain the cooked pasta and rinse it well under cold running water. Drain the pasta again and toss it with the pepper and vinegar.

To prepare the pesto, purée the celery leaves, 2 tablespoons of the pistachios, the oil, garlic and stock in a blender or food processor, scraping down the sides from time to time. Add the Parmesan and blend the mixture just enough to incorporate the cheese.

Pour the pesto over the pasta and toss well. Garnish the salad with the reserved celery leaves and the remaining pistachios. Serve cold.

Asian Pasta and Garter Bean Salad

Serves 8 as a side dish
Working (and total) time: about 30 minutes

Calories **150**
Protein **5g**
Cholesterol **0mg**
Total fat **3g**
Saturated fat **0g**
Sodium **20mg**

250 g	dried Asian wheat noodles (somen) or dried vermicelli	8 oz
250 g	garter beans or French beans, trimmed and cut into 6 cm (2½ inch) lengths	8 oz
3	spring onions, trimmed, finely chopped	3
1 tbsp	finely chopped fresh coriander	1 tbsp
1 tbsp	roasted, unsalted peanuts, chopped	1 tbsp
Celery-sesame dressing		
60 g	celery, chopped	2 oz
45 g	onion, chopped	1½ oz
2 tbsp	rice vinegar	2 tbsp
1 tbsp	safflower oil	1 tbsp
1 tbsp	low-sodium soy sauce or shoyu	1 tbsp
1 tbsp	finely chopped fresh ginger root	1 tbsp
1 tsp	dark sesame oil	1 tsp
1	clove garlic, finely chopped	1
2 tbsp	fresh lemon juice	2 tbsp
¼ tsp	chili paste	¼ tsp

Bring 4 litres (7 pints) of water to the boil in a large pan. Add the pasta and cook it until it is *al dente* — 3 to 5 minutes. Drain the pasta and rinse it under cold water. Transfer it to a large bowl of cold water and set aside.

Bring 2 litres (3½ pints) of water to the boil in a large saucepan. Add the beans and blanch them until just tender — about 3 minutes. Drain and refresh the beans under cold running water. Drain and set aside.

To make the dressing, put the celery, onion, vinegar, safflower oil, soy sauce, ginger, sesame oil, garlic, lemon juice and chili paste into a blender or food processor. Purée the dressing until it is smooth.

Drain the pasta well and transfer it to a bowl. Pour in the dressing, spring onions and coriander, and toss. Heap the dressed noodles or vermicelli in the centre of a platter or serving dish, then poke the beans one at a time into the mound to form a sunburst pattern. Sprinkle on the peanuts. Serve the salad at once.

Spirals with Spring Vegetables

Serves 8 as a first course
Working time: about 40 minutes
Total time: about 1 hour

Calories **170**
Protein **5g**
Cholesterol **0mg**
Total fat **4g**
Saturated fat **1g**
Sodium **175mg**

¼ litre	unsalted chicken or vegetable stock	8 fl oz
250 g	fresh shiitake mushrooms or field mushrooms, wiped clean and cut into 1 cm (½ inch) pieces	8 oz
1	large onion (about 250 g/8 oz), halved, each half quartered	1
½ tsp	salt	½ tsp
2 tbsp	virgin olive oil	2 tbsp
4 tbsp	red wine vinegar	4 tbsp
3	carrots	3
2 tbsp	fresh lemon juice	2 tbsp
250 g	asparagus, trimmed and sliced diagonally into 2.5 cm (1 inch) lengths	8 oz
250 g	pasta spirals or other fancy pasta	8 oz
4 tbsp	thinly sliced fresh basil leaves	4 tbsp
	freshly ground black pepper	

Heat 17.5 cl (6 fl oz) of the stock in a large, non-reactive sauté pan over medium heat. Add the mushrooms, onion chunks and ¼ teaspoon of the salt. Bring the mixture to a simmer, reduce the heat to low, and cover the pan. Cook the vegetables for 5 minutes. Remove the lid and continue cooking the vegetables, stirring frequently, until all the stock has evaporated. Stir in 1 tablespoon of the olive oil and cook the mixture for 3 minutes more.

Transfer the contents of the pan to a large bowl and return the pan to the stove over low heat. Pour the vinegar and the remaining stock into the pan. Simmer the liquid, scraping the bottom of the pan with a wooden spoon to dislodge any pan deposits, until only 2 tablespoons of liquid remain. Stir the reduced liquid into the mushrooms and onions in the bowl; set the bowl aside.

Bring 2 litres (3½ pints) of water to the boil in a

saucepan. While the water heats, prepare the carrots: cut off the tip of each one at an oblique angle. Roll the carrot a quarter or third turn, and with the knife still at the same angle, cut again. Continue rolling and cutting until you near the end of the carrot.

Add to the boiling water 1 tablespoon of the lemon juice, ¼ teaspoon of salt and the roll-cut carrots. Boil the carrots until they are barely tender — about 6 minutes. Add the asparagus pieces and boil them for 30 seconds. With a slotted spoon, transfer the vegetables to a colander; do not discard the cooking liquid. Refresh the carrots and asparagus under cold running water; when thoroughly cooled, drain them well and toss them with the mushrooms and onions. Refrigerate the vegetables while you finish the salad.

Return the water in the saucepan to a full boil; add the pasta and the remaining lemon juice. Start testing the pasta for doneness after 10 minutes and cook it until it is *al dente*. Drain the pasta and rinse it under cold running water. Drain it again.

Add the pasta to the vegetables along with the remaining olive oil, the basil, the remaining salt and a generous grinding of pepper. Toss the salad well and chill it for 10 minutes before serving.

Chilled Rice Noodle Salad

Serves 4 as a main course at lunch
Working time: about 15 minutes
Total time: about 1 hour (includes chilling)

Calories **375**
Protein **14g**
Cholesterol **25mg**
Total fat **10g**
Saturated fat **3g**
Sodium **210mg**

175 g	boneless pork loin, julienned	6 oz
4 tbsp	rice vinegar	4 tbsp
1 tbsp	finely chopped garlic	1 tbsp
1 tbsp	finely chopped fresh ginger root	1 tbsp
2 tsp	Chinese five-spice powder	2 tsp
4 tbsp	cream sherry	4 tbsp
250 g	mange-tout, stems and strings removed	8 oz
1 tbsp	safflower oil	1 tbsp
250 g	dried rice noodles	8 oz
¼ tsp	salt	¼ tsp
	freshly ground black pepper	
½ tsp	dark sesame oil	½ tsp

Put the pork in a small heatproof bowl and set it aside. Combine the vinegar, garlic, ginger, five-spice powder and sherry in a small saucepan, and bring the mixture to a simmer. Pour the marinade over the pork and let it cool to room temperature — about 15 minutes.

Meanwhile, blanch the mange-tout for 30 seconds. Refresh them under cold running water, then drain them well and transfer them to a large bowl.

Drain the pork, reserving the marinade for the dressing. Heat the safflower oil in a heavy frying pan over medium-high heat. Add the pork and sauté it until it loses its pink hue — 3 to 4 minutes. With a slotted spoon, transfer the pork to the bowl containing the mange-tout. Pour the reserved marinade into the frying pan and bring it to the boil; cook the marinade for 1 minute. Remove the frying pan from the heat and set it aside.

Add the noodles to 3 litres (5 pints) of boiling water ▶

with 1 teaspoon of salt. Start testing the noodles for doneness after 4 minutes and cook them until they are *al dente*. Drain the noodles and rinse them under cold running water; drain them again and add them to the pork and mange-tout. Pour the reserved pork marinade over the noodle mixture, then add the ¼ teaspoon of salt, some pepper and the sesame oil. Toss the salad well and refrigerate it for at least 20 minutes before serving it.

EDITOR'S NOTE: *A variation of Chinese five-spice powder may be made at home by chopping in a blender equal parts of Sichuan peppercorns, fennel seeds, ground cloves and ground cinnamon.*

Wagon-Wheel Pasta Salad

Serves 12 as a first course
Working (and total) time: about 35 minutes

Calories **210**
Protein **7g**
Cholesterol **0mg**
Total fat **4g**
Saturated fat **1g**
Sodium **170mg**

8	sun-dried tomatoes	8
500 g	wagon wheels or other fancy pasta	1 lb
300 g	fresh shelled broad beans, skinned, or frozen broad beans thawed	10 oz
2	garlic cloves, peeled	2
4 tbsp	red wine vinegar	4 tbsp
¼ tsp	salt	¼ tsp
	freshly ground black pepper	
2 tbsp	cut chives	2 tbsp
4	cherry tomatoes, cut into quarters	4
1 tbsp	virgin olive oil	1 tbsp

Put the sun-dried tomatoes into a small heatproof bowl and pour 12.5 cl (4 fl oz) of boiling water over them. Let the tomatoes soak for 20 minutes.

While the tomatoes are soaking, add the pasta to 4 litres (7 pints) of boiling water with 1 teaspoon of salt. Begin testing for doneness after 5 minutes and cook it until it is *al dente*. Drain the pasta and rinse it under cold running water; drain it once more and transfer

the pasta to a large bowl. Add the fresh broad beans to 1 litre (1¾ pints) of boiling water and cook them until barely tender — 8 to 10 minutes. Drain the beans and set them aside. (If you are using frozen beans, cook them in 4 tablespoons of boiling water for 5 minutes.)

In a blender or food processor, purée the sun-dried tomatoes along with their soaking liquid, the garlic, vinegar, salt and some pepper. Add the broad beans, chives, cherry tomatoes, oil and tomato-garlic purée to the pasta; toss well and serve the salad immediately.

Pasta Salad with Black Bean Sauce

Serves 8 as a main course at lunch
Working time: about 15 minutes
Total time: about 1 hour and 30 minutes
(includes chilling)

Calories **290**
Protein **12g**
Cholesterol **0mg**
Total fat **7g**
Saturated fat **1g**
Sodium **495mg**

500 g	vermicelli (or other thin pasta)	1 lb
2 tbsp	peanut oil	2 tbsp
2	small dried hot red chili peppers, coarsely chopped (caution, page 17)	2
3	spring onions, trimmed and sliced diagonally	3
2	garlic cloves, finely chopped	2
30 g	fermented black beans, rinsed	1 oz
250 g	firm tofu, cut into 2 cm (¾ inch) cubes	8 oz
12.5 cl	unsalted chicken stock	4 fl oz
2	celery sticks, sliced diagonally	2
¼ tsp	salt	¼ tsp
4 tsp	rice vinegar	4 tsp

Add the vermicelli with 1 teaspoon of salt to 4 litres (7 pints) of boiling water. Start testing the pasta after 5

minutes and cook it until it is *al dente*. Drain the pasta, transfer it to a large bowl of cold water, and set it aside while you make the sauce.

To begin the sauce, heat the peanut oil and chili peppers in a small saucepan; when the oil begins to smoke, remove the pan from the heat and set it aside to cool for about 5 minutes. Strain the oil into a heavy frying pan. Discard the chili peppers.

Put the spring onions and garlic into the pan containing the peanut oil; cook them over medium heat for 2 minutes. Add the black beans, tofu and stock, and simmer the mixture for 5 minutes. Stir in the celery and salt, and continue cooking the mixture until the celery is barely tender about 2 minutes more.

While the sauce is simmering, drain the noodles well. Transfer the noodles to a large bowl and toss them with the vinegar. Pour the hot sauce over all and mix thoroughly. Refrigerate the salad for at least 1 hour before serving.

Buckwheat Noodle Salad

Serves 8 as a first course
Working (and total) time: about 25 minutes

Calories **130**
Protein **3g**
Cholesterol **0mg**
Total fat **3g**
Saturated fat **0g**
Sodium **135mg**

250 g	dried buckwheat noodles (soba)	8 oz
1	sweet red pepper, seeded, deribbed and julienned	1
3	Chinese cabbage leaves, torn in small pieces	3
Ginger-lime dressing		
2.5 cm	piece fresh ginger root, peeled and coarsely chopped	1 inch
1	lime, rind grated and juice reserved	1
¼ tsp	salt	¼ tsp
½ tsp	honey	½ tsp
1	small shallot, finely chopped	1
1½ tbsp	safflower oil	1½ tbsp
½ tsp	dark sesame oil	½ tsp

Add the noodles to 2 litres (3½ pints) of boiling water in a large saucepan. Start testing them for doneness after 5 minutes and cook them until they are *al dente*. Drain the noodles and rinse them well; then cover them with cold water and set them aside.

To make the dressing, place the ginger, lime rind and salt in a mortar; mash them with a pestle until the ginger is reduced to very small pieces. Stir in the lime juice, honey, shallot and two oils. Drain the noodles and transfer them to a serving platter. Pour the dressing over them and toss them with the pepper strips. Serve immediately, surrounded by the cabbage.

Ditalini Salad with Smoked Salmon

Serves 8 as a first course or side dish
Working time: about 20 minutes
Total time: about 30 minutes

Calories **130**
Protein **5g**
Cholesterol **3mg**
Total fat **1g**
Saturated fat **0g**
Sodium **110mg**

250 g	ditalini or elbow macaroni	8 oz
12.5 cl	plain low-fat yogurt	4 fl oz
1 tbsp	brown sugar	1 tbsp
¾ tsp	dry mustard	¾ tsp
2 tbsp	cut fresh dill	2 tbsp
2 tbsp	fresh lemon juice	2 tbsp
¼ tsp	salt	¼ tsp
	freshly ground black pepper	
30 g	smoked salmon, cut into 5mm (¼ inch) cubes	1 oz

Add the pasta to 4 litres (7 pints) of boiling water with 1½ teaspoons of salt. Begin testing the pasta after 5 minutes and cook it until it is *al dente*. Drain the pasta and rinse it under cold running water; drain it once more and transfer it to a large bowl.

To prepare the dressing, whisk together the yogurt, brown sugar, mustard, dill, lemon juice, salt and some pepper in a small bowl.

Add the salmon to the pasta, pour the dressing over all, and toss well; serve the salad immediately.

EDITOR'S NOTE: *Both the dressing and pasta may be prepared 1 hour before serving time; they should be refrigerated separately and assembled at the last possible moment.*

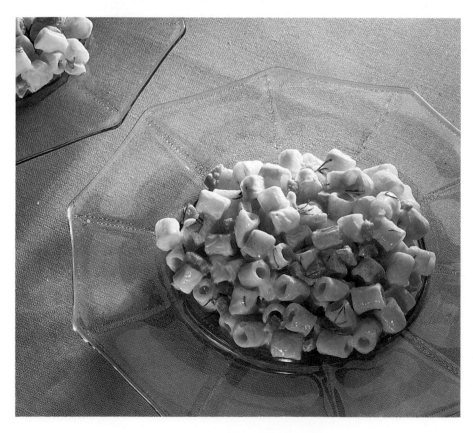

Pasta Salad with Tomato-Anchovy Sauce

Serves 6 as a side dish
Working time: about 1 hour and 15 minutes
Total time: about 2 hours and 15 minutes

Calories **135**
Protein **4g**
Cholesterol **0mg**
Total fat **3g**
Saturated fat **0g**
Sodium **45mg**

1 tbsp	virgin olive oil	1 tbsp
4 tbsp	finely chopped red onion	4 tbsp
1	garlic clove, finely chopped	1
½ tsp	paprika, preferably Hungarian	½ tsp
¼ tsp	cinnamon	¼ tsp
¼ tsp	ground cumin	¼ tsp
	cayenne pepper	
	freshly ground black pepper	
750 g	ripe tomatoes, skinned, seeded and chopped	1½ lb
2	anchovies, rinsed, patted dry with paper towels and cut into pieces	2
1 tsp	red wine vinegar	1 tsp
125 g	small carrots, peeled and cut into bâtonnets	4 oz
125 g	French beans, trimmed and cut into 4 cm (1½ inch) lengths	4 oz
2	sweet yellow or red peppers	2
125 g	penne or ziti	4 oz
2 tbsp	chopped fresh basil	2 tbsp

To prepare the tomato sauce, heat the oil in a large, heavy frying pan over medium heat. Add the onion and garlic and sauté them, stirring frequently, until the onion is translucent — about 5 minutes. Add the paprika, cinnamon, cumin, a pinch of cayenne pepper and some black pepper; continue sautéing, stirring constantly, for 30 seconds. Stir in the tomatoes and anchovy pieces, and raise the heat to medium high. Bring the sauce to a simmer and cook it, stirring frequently, until it is thickened — about 12 minutes. Remove the pan from the heat and stir in the vinegar. Set the sauce aside and let it cool thoroughly.

Meanwhile, cook the vegetables: pour enough water into a saucepan to fill it about 2.5 cm (1 inch) deep. Set a vegetable steamer in the pan and bring the water to the boil. Put the carrots and beans into the steamer, cover, and steam the vegetables until they are tender — 2 to 3 minutes. Refresh them under cold running water; drain and set aside.

Roast the yellow or red peppers about 5 cm (2 inches) below a preheated grill, turning them until they are blistered on all sides. Place the peppers in a bowl and cover the bowl with plastic film; the trapped steam will loosen their skins. Peel and seed the peppers, then cut them into 1 cm (½ inch) squares.

Add the pasta to 2 litres (3½ pints) of boiling water with ½ teaspoon of salt. Start testing the pasta after 8 minutes and cook it until it is *al dente*. Drain the pasta and rinse it under cold running water, then drain it again. Transfer the pasta to a large bowl. Add the tomato sauce along with the carrots, beans, pepper pieces and basil; toss the salad well. Let the salad stand at room temperature for 1 hour before serving it.

3 The basic materials of meat and seafood salads set the stage for fresh herbs to play their roles as complements and counterpoints.

The Ingredients of Success

Any book as full of vegetable-based recipes as this one should, for the sake of balance, include salads made with meat, poultry, fish and shellfish. Not only is there pure eating pleasure to recommend them; there is also the nutrition they provide. Saltwater fish and shellfish contribute iodine, phosphorus and other valuable minerals to the diet; both meat and poultry rank high in the various B vitamins and iron.

Almost any recipe in this section is worthy of star billing on the table. If many take longer to prepare than some in the preceding sections, they repay the extra time spent on them, since most can be served as main courses. Beautifully garnished or artfully arranged, they will satisfy the eye, please the appetite, and delight guests or family. Moreover, they make for cool summer eating when hot food can seem too much of a good thing.

If you plan to serve the salads as main courses, you may wish to supplement them with bread, rolls or other starchy foods, and you may want to include another salad, perhaps one made of leafy greens or of vegetables for additional fibre, vitamins and minerals.

The dishes are calculated to be healthy. Pork and lamb, two meats generally not associated with salads, are used, as well as beef. The cuts are lean, and any visible fat is removed; cooking the meat slowly by such methods as roasting, braising and poaching guarantees that fat will be rendered from the tissue; the fat can then be skimmed from the cooking liquid. Poultry is skinned to remove fat and cooked gently to preserve succulence and flavour.

The recipes are also innovative. In a departure from tradition, a fish terrine — usually presented in solitary splendour as a first course — serves as the focus of an elegant salad. In another, vegetables are roasted with shellfish in a little oil and served tender but still crisp. Meat is sometimes added to the salads in slices, rather than in pieces. To enhance the flavour of the salads themselves, the cooking juices are often blended into the dressings. And when it comes to some old salad stand-bys, such as turkey, chicken and crab, the inclusion of ingredients as different as peaches, barley and yogurt elevates them to new status.

Scandinavian-Style Salmon Salad

Serves 6 as a main course
Working time: about 40 minutes
Total time: about 3 hours and 15 minutes
(includes marinating)

Calories **550**
Protein **36g**
Cholesterol **115mg**
Total fat **25g**
Saturated fat **8g**
Sodium **435mg**

60 g	sugar	2 oz
30 cl	white wine vinegar	½ pint
2	small red onions, thinly sliced	2
	freshly ground black pepper	
½ tsp	mustard seeds	½ tsp
2	bay leaves	2
6	tail-end of salmon steaks (about 1 kg/2¼ lb)	6
500 g	potatoes, peeled and sliced	1 lb
3	carrots, sliced into thin rounds	3
2 tbsp	chopped fresh dill, or 2 tsp dried dill	2 tbsp
1	small cucumber	1
6	radishes, thinly sliced	6
1	large round lettuce, washed and dried	1
Rye toast		
30 g	unsalted butter	1 oz
2 tbsp	grated red onion	2 tbsp
½ tsp	caraway seeds	½ tsp
12	slices dark rye bread	12

Put the sugar, vinegar, half of the onions, some pepper, the mustard seeds and the bay leaves into a small, non-reactive saucepan. Bring the liquid to the boil, reduce the heat, and simmer the marinade for 10 minutes.

Set the salmon steaks in a non-reactive heatproof dish large enough to hold them in a single layer. Strain the marinade over them, discarding the solids. Simmer the fish over medium heat for 2 minutes. Remove the dish from the heat and allow it to cool to room temperature — about 30 minutes.

Pour enough water into a saucepan to fill it about 2.5 cm (1 inch) deep. Set a vegetable steamer in the pan and bring the water to the boil. Put the potatoes into the steamer, cover the pan tightly, and steam the potatoes until they are tender — about 6 minutes. Add the potatoes to the fish. Steam the carrots in the same way, but for only 3 minutes. Add the carrots to the fish and potatoes. Sprinkle the dill over the fish and vegetables, cover the dish, and refrigerate the mixture for at least 2 hours.

Shortly before serving the salad, score the cucumber lengthwise with a cannelle knife or a paring knife. Slice the cucumber into thin rounds and add them to the fish along with the radishes and the remaining onion.

To make the toast, first preheat the oven to 230°C (450°F or Mark 8). Mix together the butter, grated onion, caraway seeds and some pepper. Spread this mixture on the rye bread slices, then toast them in the oven on a baking sheet for about 4 minutes.

Using a slotted spoon, transfer the salad to a serving dish lined with the lettuce leaves. Pour about half the marinade over the salad; discard the remainder. Serve the salad accompanied by the rye toast.

Seviche Salad

THIS RECIPE CALLS FOR 4 TABLESPOONS OF SUGAR; IT IS ADDED TO THE WATER USED FOR BLANCHING ORANGE RIND, THEN DISCARDED.

Serves 8 as a main course
Working time: about 45 minutes
Total time: about one day (includes marinating time)

Calories **210**
Protein **22g**
Cholesterol **45mg**
Total fat **7g**
Saturated fat **1g**
Sodium **380mg**

4	oranges	4
4 tbsp	sugar	4 tbsp
3	limes	3
3	lemons	3
3	sticks celery, thinly sliced	3
1	sweet green pepper, seeded, deribbed and julienned	1
1	sweet yellow pepper, seeded, deribbed and julienned	1
1	small red onion, thinly sliced	1
1	garlic clove, finely chopped	1
2 tbsp	chopped fresh coriander	2 tbsp
1 tsp	salt	1 tsp
½ tsp	black pepper	½ tsp
	Tabasco sauce	
½ tsp	ground cumin	½ tsp
¼ tsp	cumin seeds	¼ tsp
500 g	scallops, the bright, white connective tissue removed, the scallops rinsed and patted dry	1 lb
500 g	halibut fillets, rinsed, patted dry and cut into 1 cm (½ inch) cubes	1 lb
125 g	spinach, washed, stemmed and dried, or 1 oakleaf lettuce, washed and dried	4 oz
2 tbsp	chopped parsley, preferably flat-leaf	2 tbsp
2 tbsp	virgin olive oil	2 tbsp

Using a vegetable peeler, remove the rind from one orange, leaving behind as much of the pith as possible. Cut the rind into fine julienne, then put it into a small saucepan with 35 cl (12 fl oz) of water and the sugar. Bring the water to the boil and cook the rind for 2 minutes. Drain the rind and transfer it to a large, non-reactive bowl. Into another bowl, squeeze the juice from the oranges, limes and lemons, strain it and set it aside.

Add the celery, green and yellow peppers, onion, garlic, coriander, salt, pepper, a few drops of Tabasco sauce, the ground cumin and cumin seeds to the bowl. Gently toss the contents of the bowl with the scallops and the halibut cubes. Pour the citrus juices over all and toss again. Press down on the solid ingredients so that they are completely submerged. Cover the bowl and let the seviche marinate in the refrigerator for 8 hours.

Use a slotted spoon to transfer the seviche to a platter or individual plates lined with the spinach or lettuce. Pour 12.5 cl (4 fl oz) of the marinade into a small bowl. Add the parsley; then, whisking constantly, pour in the oil in a slow, steady stream. Spoon the dressing over the salad and serve immediately.

generous grinding of black pepper; set the bowl aside.

To prepare the dressing, combine the mustard, the dill, some pepper and the tablespoon of lemon juice in a small bowl. Whisking vigorously, pour in the oil in a thin, steady stream; continue whisking until the dressing is thoroughly combined, then set the bowl aside.

Add the linguine with ½ teaspoon of salt to 4 litres (7 pints) of boiling water. Start testing the pasta for doneness after 8 minutes and cook until *al dente*. Drain the pasta and rinse it under cold running water, then transfer it to a large bowl and toss it with half of the dressing; set aside.

Pour enough water into a wok or large shallow pan to fill it about 2.5 cm (1 inch) deep. Put the julienned vegetables in a bamboo steamer and set the steamer in the wok or pan. (If you lack a bamboo steamer, steam the vegetables on a plate set on a wire rack in the bottom of a large pan.) Bring the water to the boil, tightly cover the wok or pan, and steam the vegetables for about 1 minute. Place the fish pieces on top of the vegetables, cover the pan again and steam the fish until it is opaque and feels firm to the touch — 1 to 2 minutes. Remove the steamer or plate and let the fish and vegetables cool.

Mound the linguine on a serving platter. Top the pasta with the cooled fish and vegetables. Pour the remaining dressing over the salad and serve immediately.

Monkfish Salad with Green and White Linguine

Serves 4 as a main course
Working time: about 50 minutes
Total time: about 1 hour and 15 minutes

Calories **440**
Protein **30g**
Cholesterol **45mg**
Total fat **10g**
Saturated fat **1g**
Sodium **290mg**

500 g	monkfish fillets, rinsed, patted dry and cut into 2.5 by 5 cm (1 by 2 inch) pieces	1 lb
1	lemon, juice only	1
1 tbsp	chopped fresh thyme, or 1 tsp dried thyme	1 tbsp
⅛ tsp	cayenne pepper	⅛ tsp
¼ tsp	salt	¼ tsp
	freshly ground black pepper	
2	leeks, trimmed, split, washed thoroughly to remove all grit, and julienned	2
1	carrot, julienned	1
1	stick celery, julienned	1
125 g	spinach linguine or narrow fettuccine	4 oz
125 g	linguine or narrow fettuccine	4 oz
Dill dressing		
½ tsp	Dijon mustard	½ tsp
1 tbsp	finely cut fresh dill, or 2 tsp dried dill	1 tbsp
	freshly ground black pepper	
1 tbsp	fresh lemon juice	1 tbsp
2 tbsp	safflower oil	2 tbsp

Place the fish pieces in a shallow dish. In a small bowl, combine the juice of the lemon with the thyme, cayenne pepper, salt and some black pepper. Pour the lemon marinade over the fish and let the fish marinate for at least 30 minutes.

Toss the leek, carrot and celery in a bowl with a

Chilled Fish Salad with Okra

Serves 4 as a main course
Working time: about 45 minutes
Total time: about 1 hour and 45 minutes

Calories **350**
Protein **26g**
Cholesterol **50mg**
Total fat **9g**
Saturated fat **1g**
Sodium **235mg**

1	bunch spring onions, trimmed, green parts left whole, white parts thinly sliced	1
3	bay leaves	3
¼ litre	red wine vinegar	8 fl oz
500 g	thin cod fillets, rinsed and cut crosswise into pieces about 7.5 cm (3 inches) long	1 lb
2 tbsp	tomato paste	2 tbsp
750 g	large ripe tomatoes, skinned, seeded and coarsely chopped	1½ lb
2 tsp	sugar	2 tsp
¼ tsp	salt	¼ tsp
3 tbsp	chopped parsley	3 tbsp
2 tbsp	chopped fresh oregano, or 2 tsp dried oregano	2 tbsp
500 g	fresh peas, shelled, or 150 g (5 oz) frozen peas, thawed	1 lb
165 g	fresh sweetcorn kernels (from about 1 large ear), or frozen sweetcorn kernels, thawed	5½ oz
175 g	okra, trimmed and cut into 1 cm (½ inch) rounds	6 oz
2 tbsp	safflower oil	2 tbsp
125 g	cornmeal	4 oz
1 tbsp	cayenne pepper	1 tbsp

Pour 1.5 litres (2½ pints) of water into a large, non-reactive saucepan set over medium heat. Add the spring onion greens, bay leaves and 12.5 cl (4 fl oz) of the vinegar, and simmer the liquid for 15 minutes.

Arrange the fish pieces in a single layer in a shallow dish. Strain the hot liquid over the fish; let the dish stand at room temperature for 20 minutes before refrigerating it for 30 minutes.

Meanwhile, whisk together the tomato paste and the remaining vinegar. Stir in the white spring onion parts, then the tomatoes, sugar, salt, parsley and oregano. Chill the relish for 30 minutes.

Pour enough water into a saucepan to fill it about 2.5 cm (1 inch) deep. Set a vegetable steamer in the pan and bring the water to the boil. Add the fresh peas to the steamer, cover the pan and cook the peas until they are just tender — 3 to 4 minutes. Add the fresh sweetcorn to the peas and steam the vegetables for 1 to 2 minutes more. (Frozen peas and sweetcorn do not require steaming but can be blanched briefly.) Transfer the peas and sweetcorn to a bowl, and chill in the refrigerator for 30 minutes.

Add the okra to the steamer and cook it for 30 seconds. Set the okra aside at room temperature.

Drain the liquid from the chilled fish. Carefully arrange a layer each of the relish, the peas and sweetcorn, and the fish in a large bowl. Top the fish with another layer of relish, then with a final layer of peas and sweetcorn.

Heat the oil in a large, heavy frying pan over medium-high heat. Combine the cornmeal with the cayenne pepper and toss the okra in this mixture; shake off the excess. Add the okra to the pan and fry it, stirring constantly, until it is brown on all sides. Scatter the okra over the salad and serve immediately.

Monkfish, Broad Bean and Red Cabbage Salad

Serves 4 as a main course
Working time: about 20 minutes
Total time: about 1 hour (includes chilling)

Calories **240**
Protein **25g**
Cholesterol **40mg**
Total fat **6g**
Saturated fat **0g**
Sodium **365mg**

500 g	monkfish fillet, trimmed, rinsed, dried	1 lb
¼ tsp	salt	¼ tsp
⅛ tsp	white pepper	⅛ tsp
300 g	fresh shelled broad beans, or frozen baby broad beans, thawed	10 oz
90 g	red cabbage, thinly sliced	3 oz
2 tbsp	chopped fresh mint, or 2 tsp dried mint	2 tbsp
3 tbsp	fish stock or unsalted chicken stock	3 tbsp
2 tbsp	sherry vinegar	2 tbsp
1 tbsp	safflower oil	1 tbsp
1 tbsp	chopped parsley	1 tbsp
1	lettuce, washed and dried	1

Cut the monkfish fillet crosswise into thin slices. Season the slices with the salt and some pepper.

Pour enough water into a saucepan to fill it about 2.5 cm (1 inch) deep. Set a vegetable steamer in the pan and bring the water to the boil. Put the monkfish slices into the steamer, tightly cover the pan, and steam the fish until it is opaque and firm to the touch — 2 to 3 minutes. Transfer the monkfish slices to a large, shallow dish.

If you are using fresh broad beans, cook them in 1 litre (1¾ pints) of boiling water until they are barely tender — 8 to 10 minutes — then drain them and add them to the monkfish. (Frozen beans require only brief blanching.) Blanch the cabbage in 1 litre (1¾ pints) of boiling water for 3 minutes; drain the cabbage and add it to the monkfish and beans.

To prepare the dressing, whisk together the mint, stock, vinegar and oil. Pour the dressing over the contents of the dish; mix the ingredients thoroughly, then refrigerate the salad for 30 minutes.

Add the parsley to the salad and toss. Serve the salad on a bed of lettuce.

Fish and Vegetable Terrine

Serves 12 as a first course
Working time: about 1 hour and 15 minutes
Total time: about 8 hours (includes chilling)

Calories **125**
Protein **10g**
Cholesterol **30mg**
Total fat **7g**
Saturated fat **1g**
Sodium **190mg**

2	shallots, chopped	2
12.5 cl	fish stock or unsalted chicken stock	4 fl oz
12	saffron threads	12
500 g	plaice fillets, rinsed, patted dry and cut into 2.5 cm (1 inch) chunks	1 lb
125 g	smoked salmon, coarsely chopped	4 oz
2	egg whites	2
5 tsp	chopped fresh tarragon, or 2½ tsp dried tarragon	5 tsp
	cayenne pepper	
12.5 cl	half milk, half cream	4 fl oz
16	French beans, trimmed	16
4	carrots, peeled and quartered lengthwise	4
12	large leaves of cos lettuce, washed	12
175 g	radicchio, washed and dried, or 2 bunches of watercress, stemmed, washed and dried	6 oz
6 tbsp	vinaigrette (recipe, page 13)	6 tbsp
1 tbsp	fresh lemon juice	1 tbsp

Put the shallots, stock and saffron into a small saucepan. Bring the mixture to a simmer and cook it for 10 minutes. Set aside to cool at room temperature.

Purée the plaice and smoked salmon in a food processor. Add the shallot mixture and purée again. With the motor running, add the egg whites, 2 teaspoons of the fresh tarragon or 1 teaspoon of the dried tarragon, and a pinch of cayenne pepper. Press the mixture through a medium sieve into a bowl. Set the bowl in a pan of ice. With a wooden spoon, incorporate the milk and cream into the fish mixture 2 tablespoons at a time. Refrigerate the mixture, covered, while you prepare the remaining ingredients.

Preheat the oven to 170°C (325°F or Mark 3).

Pour enough water into a saucepan to fill it about 2.5 cm (1 inch) deep. Set a vegetable steamer in the pan and bring the water to the boil. Put the beans into the steamer, cover the pan tightly, and steam the beans until they are tender — about 3 minutes. Remove the beans from the steamer, refresh them under cold running water, drain them, and set aside. Steam the carrots the same way until tender — about 6 minutes. Refresh and drain the carrots and set aside.

Bring a large pan of water to the boil. Blanch the lettuce leaves in the boiling water until they are limp — about 1 minute. Remove the leaves with a slotted spoon and drain them on paper towels. When the leaves are cool enough to handle, use a paring knife to trim away the thickest part of each leaf's centre rib.

Lightly oil a 1.25 litre (2 pint) ceramic or glass terrine. Line it with the lettuce leaves, overlapping them slightly. Allow the tips to overhang the sides; the tips will later be folded over to enclose the fish and vegetables. ▶

Spread one quarter of the fish purée in the bottom of the terrine. Arrange half of the carrot quarters on top of the purée and parallel to the terrine's sides, leaving a 1 cm (½ inch) border uncovered round the edge.

Spread one third of the remaining purée over the carrots, covering them entirely. Arrange the beans in a single layer in the terrine as you did the first layer of carrots. Spread half of the remaining fish over the beans; arrange another layer of carrots on top of the purée and finish the assembly with the remaining fish. Fold over the lettuce leaves to encase the layers snugly. Rap the terrine sharply on the work surface to eliminate any trapped air pockets.

Cover the terrine with aluminium foil. Using a skewer, poke two holes in the foil; set the terrine in a roasting pan filled half way with boiling water. Transfer the pan to the oven and bake the terrine for 1 hour. Remove the roasting pan from the oven and let the terrine rest, still in the roasting pan, for 1 hour. Remove the terrine from the roasting pan and refrigerate it for 5 hours before serving it.

To unmould, cover the terrine with a small cutting board and turn both over together; gently lift away the terrine dish. Slice the unmoulded terrine into 12 serving pieces. Arrange the radicchio or watercress on 12 individual plates; set a slice of terrine on each plate. Whisk together the vinaigrette, the remaining tarragon and the lemon juice. Dribble a little of the dressing over each portion and serve at once.

Fish Rolled in Nori

Serves 6 as a first course
Working time: about 25 minutes
Total time: about 40 minutes

Calories **115**
Protein **14g**
Cholesterol **30mg**
Total fat **4g**
Saturated fat **1g**
Sodium **105mg**

4	spring onions, trimmed	4
350 g	sole fillets, rinsed, patted dry and cut into 2.5 cm (1 inch) chunks	12 oz
1	garlic clove, chopped	1
1 tsp	finely chopped fresh ginger root	1 tsp
1	egg white	1
6	drops Tabasco sauce	6
⅛ tsp	white pepper	⅛ tsp
6 tbsp	fish stock or unsalted chicken stock	6 tbsp
3	sheets nori	3
1	large carrot, cut into 5 cm (2 inch) segments, each halved lengthwise and cut into 5 mm (¼ inch) thick strips	1
125 g	lamb's lettuce (corn salad), washed and dried, or spinach, washed, stemmed and dried	4 oz
2 tbsp	mirin (sweet Japanese rice wine)	2 tbsp
1 tbsp	rice vinegar	1 tbsp
¼ tsp	dark sesame oil	¼ tsp
1 tbsp	peanut oil	1 tbsp

Cut the green tops off the spring onions and julienne enough of them to yield about 1 tablespoon. Set the julienne aside. Coarsely chop the white parts of the spring onions and transfer them to a food processor or a blender. Add the fish chunks, garlic, ginger, egg white, Tabasco sauce, white pepper and stock; purée the mixture, pausing occasionally to scrape down the sides, until no large pieces of fish remain.

Place a sheet of nori, shiny side down, on a work surface. Spread 6 tablespoons of the fish mixture along one of the shorter edges of the sheet, forming a ribbon about 2.5 cm (1 inch) wide. Lay a line of carrot strips end to end down the centre of the ribbon. Press down lightly on the carrot strips to anchor them in the mixture. Starting at the edge with the purée on it, roll up the nori to enclose the fish mixture. Cut off the excess nori — about half a sheet — and use it to make another fish roll. Use the remaining nori sheets, fish mixture and carrot strips to fashion a total of six rolls.

Pour enough water into a deep frying pan to fill it to a depth of about 5 cm (2 inches). Bring the water to the boil, then reduce the heat to maintain a gentle simmer. Lower the nori rolls into the water and poach them until the fish is cooked — 4 to 5 minutes. To test for doneness, gently remove a roll from the water with a slotted spoon and cut a slice from each end; the fish purée should be opaque. Remove the rolls from the water and allow them to cool to room temperature, then slice them into rounds about 1 cm (½ inch) thick. Arrange a line of rounds on each plate with lamb's lettuce or spinach on either side.

Whisk together the mirin, rice vinegar, sesame oil, and peanut oil; pour some dressing over each portion. Garnish with the spring onion julienne and serve at once.

Trout Salad
with Basil Vinaigrette

Serves 4 as a first course
Working time: about 20 minutes
Total time: about 40 minutes

Calories **200**
Protein **22g**
Cholesterol **65mg**
Total fat **10g**
Saturated fat **1g**
Sodium **185mg**

2	trout (500 g/1 lb each), filleted	2
2 tbsp	sherry vinegar	2 tbsp
1 tbsp	finely chopped shallot	1 tbsp
1	small garlic clove, finely chopped	1
¼ tsp	salt	¼ tsp
⅛ tsp	white pepper	⅛ tsp
1 tbsp	safflower oil	1 tbsp
4 tbsp	loosely packed fresh basil leaves, cut into chiffonade (page 51)	4 tbsp
2	ripe tomatoes, each cut into 6 slices	2
4	sprigs fresh basil	4

Lay a trout fillet on a cutting board with its skinned side down. With a small knife, cut along one side of the line of bones running the length of the fillet. Make a similar cut along the other side of the line of bones; discard the thin strip of flesh and bones thus formed. You

should now have two pieces, one twice the width of the other. Halve the larger piece lengthwise. Fold each piece into a loose "bow" and set the bow on a heat-proof plate. Repeat these steps to fashion the remaining fillets into bows.

Pour enough water into a large pan to fill it about 2.5 cm (1 inch) deep. Place two or three small bowls of equal height in the bottom of the pan; set the plate on top of the bowls. Cover the pan, bring the water to the boil, and steam the fish until it is opaque and firm to the touch — about 2 minutes. Remove the plate and set it aside while you prepare the dressing.

Whisk together the vinegar, shallot, garlic, salt, pepper, oil and half of the basil. Pour this dressing over the fish bows and refrigerate them until they are cool — about 20 minutes.

Arrange three tomato slices on each of four plates. Use a spatula to transfer a bow on to each tomato slice. Sprinkle the salads with the remaining chiffonade of basil. Dribble the chilled dressing over all, garnish with the basil sprigs, and serve at once.

Lobster Salad
with Sweet Peppers
and Coriander

Serves 4 as a main course or 8 as a first course
Working time: about 30 minutes
Total time: about 2 hours and 30 minutes
(includes chilling and marinating)

Calories **190**
Protein **18g**
Cholesterol **65mg**
Total fat **8g**
Saturated fat **1g**
Sodium **250mg**

2	carrots, sliced into thin rounds	2
1	onion, thinly sliced	1
6 tbsp	coarsely chopped parsley, stems included	6 tbsp
2	bay leaves	2
8	black peppercorns	8
1 tbsp	vinegar, wine or lemon juice	1 tbsp
3	live lobsters (about 600 g/1¼ lb each)	3
2 tbsp	fresh lemon juice	2 tbsp
2 tbsp	fresh lime juice	2 tbsp
2 tbsp	virgin olive oil	2 tbsp
1	sweet red pepper, seeded, deribbed and cut into 5 mm (¼ inch) dice	1
1	sweet yellow pepper, seeded, deribbed and cut into 5 mm (¼ inch) dice	1
½	cucumber, seeded and cut into bâtonnets	½
½	small red onion, chopped	½
1½ tbsp	chopped fresh coriander	1½ tbsp
	freshly ground black pepper	
4 or 8	large red-leaf lettuce leaves, washed and dried	4 or 8
8 or 16	thin lemon wedges	8 or 16

Pour enough water into a large cooking pot to fill it about 2.5 cm (1 inch) deep. Add the carrots, onion, parsley, bay leaves, peppercorns and vinegar, wine or lemon juice. Bring the liquid to the boil, then reduce the heat and simmer the mixture for 20 minutes. Return the liquid to the boil, add the lobsters, and cover the pot; cook the lobsters until they turn a bright

red-orange — about 15 minutes. Remove the lobsters and let them cool. When the lobsters are cool enough to handle, remove the claw and tail meat and cut the tail meat into 2 cm (¾ inch) slices.

Combine the lemon and lime juices in a large bowl, then whisk in the oil. Add the lobster meat, peppers, cucumber, red onion, coriander and some pepper. Toss the mixture well, then cover the bowl. Refrigerate the salad for at least 2 hours to meld the flavours,

stirring several times to distribute the dressing.

To serve, place a lettuce leaf on each plate; divide the lobster salad among the plates, then garnish each salad with two lemon wedges.

EDITOR'S NOTE: *If you like, the lobster-cooking liquid may be strained and reserved for another use — as a medium for boiling pasta, or as the base for a seafood stew. To give the liquid even more flavour, simmer the lobster shells in it for 20 minutes before straining it.*

Thai Lemon-Lime Prawn Salad

Serves 4 as a main course at lunch
Working (and total) time: about 45 minutes

Calories **125**
Protein **18g**
Cholesterol **130mg**
Total fat **1g**
Saturated fat **0g**
Sodium **230mg**

1	tart green apple, preferably Granny Smith, peeled, cored and julienned	1
3 tbsp	fresh lemon juice	3 tbsp
3 tbsp	fresh lime juice	3 tbsp
2	shallots, thinly sliced	2
1½ tbsp	chopped fresh coriander	1½ tbsp
1 tbsp	chopped fresh mint, or 1 tsp dried mint	1 tbsp
2 tsp	fish sauce, or low-sodium soy sauce	2 tsp
2	garlic cloves, finely chopped	2
1	small dried red chili pepper, soaked in hot water for 20 minutes, drained, seeded and chopped (caution, page 17)	1
2	spring onions, thinly sliced	2
500 g	large, freshly cooked prawns, peeled, deveined if necessary and halved	1 lb
2	large round lettuces, washed and dried	2
4	mint sprigs	4

Put the julienned apple into a large bowl and toss the pieces with the lemon and lime juices, shallots, coriander, mint, fish sauce or soy sauce, garlic, chili pepper and spring onions.

Add the prawns to the bowl. Gently mix them into the salad. Cover the bowl and refrigerate the salad for at least 30 minutes.

Serve the salad on lettuce leaves on individual plates, each portion garnished with a sprig of mint.

Prawn and Artichoke Salad

Serves 6 as a main course at lunch
Working (and total) time: about 1 hour and 15 minutes

Calories **140**
Protein **13g**
Cholesterol **85mg**
Total fat **5g**
Saturated fat **1g**
Sodium **70mg**

4	globe artichokes	4
1	lemon, cut in half	1
500 g	large raw prawns, peeled, and deveined if necessary	1 lb
125 g	French beans, trimmed and cut into 1 cm (½ inch) lengths	4 oz
1 kg	large ripe tomatoes, skinned, seeded and cut into 1 cm (½ inch) chunks	2 lb
2 tbsp	finely cut chives	2 tbsp
6	basil leaves, thinly sliced	6
1	garlic clove, finely chopped	1
4 tbsp	sherry vinegar or red wine vinegar	4 tbsp
1 tsp	grainy mustard	1 tsp
3 tbsp	grated onion	3 tbsp
2 tbsp	virgin olive oil	2 tbsp

Cut the stems off the artichokes. Rub the cut surfaces with one of the lemon halves to prevent discoloration.

Bring 4 litres (7 pints) of water to the boil in a large, non-reactive saucepan. Squeeze the juice of the lemon half into the water, then add the half itself. Put the artichokes into the water; reduce the heat to maintain a strong simmer, and cook the artichokes until they are tender — about 20 minutes. Remove the artichokes from the water with a slotted spoon and set them aside.

Bring 2 litres (3½ pints) of water to the boil in a non-reactive saucepan. Add the juice from the second lemon half, and drop in the rind as well. Add the prawns and cook them until they are opaque — 30 seconds to 1 minute. Drain the prawns, refresh them under cold running water, and drain them again. Reserve six of the prawns for garnish; cut the remainder into 2 cm (¾ inch) pieces. Put the prawn pieces in a large bowl.

When the artichokes are cool enough to handle, pull off their leaves. Discard the dark green outer leaves but save the inner ones for garnish. With a teaspoon, scoop the furry choke from each bottom and discard it. Cut the bottoms into 1 cm (½ inch) long pieces and add them to the prawns.

Blanch the beans in 1 litre (1¾ pints) of boiling water

until they turn bright green and are tender yet still somewhat crisp — 1 to 2 minutes. Drain the beans, refresh them under cold running water, and drain them again. Transfer the beans to the bowl containing the prawns; add the tomatoes, chives, basil and garlic.

In a small bowl, whisk together the vinegar, mustard, onion and oil. Pour this dressing over the prawns and beans, and toss well. Spoon the salad on to individual plates, garnishing each serving with the remaining artichoke leaves and one of the reserved whole prawns.

EDITOR'S NOTE: *Freshly cooked prawns can be used in this recipe instead of the raw ones.*

Prawn Salad on Fresh Pineapple-Mango Relish

Serves 8 as a main course at lunch
Working time: about 30 minutes
Total time: about 1 hour

Calories **160**	2	large ripe mangoes	2
Protein **13g**	1	pineapple, peeled and cut into 5 mm (¼ inch) cubes	1
Cholesterol **105mg**			
Total fat **4g**			
Saturated fat **1g**	4 tbsp	fresh lime juice	4 tbsp
Sodium **200mg**	30 g	fresh coriander, finely chopped	1 oz

2	sweet red peppers, halved, seeded and deribbed	2
750 g	cooked prawns, peeled, and deveined if necessary	1½ lb
4 tbsp	mayonnaise (recipe, page 13)	4 tbsp
4	spring onions, trimmed and thinly sliced	4
2 tbsp	very finely chopped fresh ginger root	2 tbsp
½ tsp	salt	½ tsp
1	fresh coriander sprig for garnish	1

To prepare the relish, first peel the mangoes and remove the flesh in pieces. Purée one quarter of the flesh in a food processor or a blender, then pass it through a sieve set over a bowl. Refrigerate the purée. Cut the remaining mango pieces into 5 mm (¼ inch) cubes and place them in a bowl. Add the pineapple, lime juice and chopped coriander; stir the relish and refrigerate it.

Dice one of the pepper halves and put the dice in a bowl with the prawns. Julienne the remaining pepper halves and set the julienne aside. Stir the mayonnaise, mango purée, spring onions, ginger and salt into the prawn-and-pepper mixture. Chill the salad in the refrigerator for at least 30 minutes.

To serve, spoon some of the pineapple-mango relish on to a large platter and surround it with some of the prawn salad. Top the relish with the remaining prawn salad; garnish the dish with the pepper julienne and the coriander sprig.

Oven-Roasted Vegetable Salad with Prawns and Scallops

Serves 4 as a main course at lunch
Working time: about 45 minutes
Total time: about 1 hour and 15 minutes

Calories **250**		
Protein **23g**		
Cholesterol **85mg**		
Total fat **9g**		
Saturated fat **1g**		
Sodium **450mg**		

250 g	shelled queen scallops, bright white connective tissue removed	8 oz
250 g	large prawns, peeled, and deveined if necessary	8 oz
7 tbsp	fresh lemon juice	7 tbsp
60 g	coarsely chopped fresh basil	2 oz
½ tsp	drained grated horseradish	½ tsp
¼ tsp	cayenne pepper	¼ tsp
250 g	mushrooms, trimmed and wiped clean	8 oz
1	small fennel bulb, thinly sliced	1
2	sticks celery, cut into 5 cm (2 inch) lengths, then into 5 mm (¼ inch) strips	2
1	carrot, cut into 5 cm (2 inch) lengths, then into 5 mm (¼ inch) strips	1
1	sweet red pepper, seeded, deribbed and cut into thin strips	1
125 g	French beans, trimmed	4 oz
4	shallots, thinly sliced	4
1 tbsp	finely chopped garlic	1 tbsp
1 tbsp	chopped fresh oregano, or 1 tsp dried oregano	1 tbsp
1 tbsp	fresh thyme, or 1 tsp dried thyme	1 tbsp
½ tsp	salt	½ tsp
2 tbsp	virgin olive oil	2 tbsp
	freshly ground black pepper	
125 g	mange-tout, stems and strings removed	4 oz
1	lettuce, washed and dried	1
1	head of chicory, leaves separated	1
2 tsp	Dijon mustard	2 tsp

1 tsp	grainy mustard	1 tsp
2 tbsp	plain low-fat yogurt	2 tbsp

Mix the scallops and the prawns with 3 tablespoons of lemon juice, the basil, horseradish and cayenne pepper. Set them aside while you roast the vegetables.

Toss the mushrooms, fennel, celery, carrot, red pepper, beans, shallots and garlic with the oregano, thyme, salt, olive oil and some black pepper. Spread the vegetables out in a single layer in a large, shallow pan and roast them in a preheated 230°C (450°F or Mark 8) oven, stirring frequently, until the shallots are translucent — 10 to 12 minutes. Add the scallops and prawns, their liquid, and the mange-tout; stir to combine all the ingredients and cook them, stirring from time to time, until the seafood is opaque — 5 to 7 minutes. Transfer the mixture to a non-reactive dish to cool at room temperature for 30 minutes.

Arrange the lettuce and chicory on a platter or individual plates. Using a slotted spoon, set the vegetables and seafood on top of the greens. Pour the liquid left in the dish into a small bowl.

Make the dressing by whisking the remaining lemon juice, Dijon mustard, grainy mustard and yogurt into the reserved liquid. Serve the dressing with the salad.

Clam Salad on Chinese Cabbage

Serves 4 as a main course
Working time: about 1 hour
Total time: about 1 hour and 30 minutes

Calories **235**		
Protein **12g**		
Cholesterol **35mg**		
Total fat **8g**		
Saturated fat **1g**		
Sodium **180mg**		

3	spring onions, trimmed and finely chopped	3
1	shallot, finely chopped	1
¼ litre	dry sherry	8 fl oz
3 tbsp	fresh lemon juice	3 tbsp
½ tsp	saffron threads	½ tsp
36	small hard-shell clams, scrubbed	36
5	round red potatoes or other waxy potatoes	5
2 tbsp	red wine vinegar	2 tbsp
1 tbsp	grainy mustard	1 tbsp
	freshly ground black pepper	
2 tbsp	safflower oil	2 tbsp
500 g	Chinese cabbage, cut into chiffonade (page 51)	1 lb
2 tbsp	thinly sliced fresh basil, or 2 tsp dried basil	2 tbsp
2 tbsp	finely chopped red onion	2 tbsp
250 g	cherry tomatoes, halved	8 oz

Combine the spring onions, shallot, sherry, lemon juice and saffron threads in a large, non-reactive pan. Bring the liquid to a simmer, then reduce the heat to low, cover the mixture, and cook it for 1 minute.

Add the clams and cover the pan. Increase the heat to medium high and cook the clams, stirring occasionally, until they open — about 3 minutes. Using a slotted spoon, transfer the clams to a large bowl; discard any clams that remain closed. Strain the clam broth through a sieve lined with muslin into a bowl, taking care not to pour any of the accumulated sand into the sieve. Rinse out the muslin and set it aside. Discard the solids.

When the clams are cool enough to handle, remove them from their shells. Dip each clam into the broth to rinse off any residual sand; reserve the broth. Place the rinsed clams in a bowl, cover the bowl, and refrigerate the clams.

Put the potatoes into a saucepan and pour in enough water to cover them by about 5 cm (2 inches). Bring the water to the boil and simmer the potatoes until they are tender — about 15 minutes. Drain them and set them aside until they are cool enough to handle.

Cut the potatoes into quarters and transfer them to a non-reactive bowl. Reline the sieve with the muslin and strain the clam broth through it. Pour the strained broth over the potatoes. Gently toss the potatoes and let them stand for 20 minutes.

Remove the potatoes from the broth and set them aside. To prepare the vinaigrette, whisk the vinegar, mustard and some pepper into the broth. Then, whisking constantly, pour in the oil in a thin, steady stream; continue whisking until the oil is fully incorporated.

Toss the cabbage with the basil, onion and about half of the vinaigrette. In a separate bowl, mix the clams and tomatoes with the remaining vinaigrette.

To assemble the salad, spread the cabbage-onion mixture on a platter. Mound the clam-and-tomato mixture in the centre and arrange the potatoes around it. Pour any remaining vinaigrette over the potatoes and serve at once.

Crab Meat Salad with Grapes and Celeriac

Serves 4 as a main course
Working time: about 1 hour
Total time: about 1 hour and 30 minutes

separate the segments from the inner membranes by slicing down to the core with a sharp knife on either side of each segment.

Mound the crab salad and the celeriac side by side on a serving platter. Garnish the salad with the orange slices and the kumquats if you are using them, and serve immediately.

Crab Salad with Spinach and Sweetcorn

Serves 6 as a main course at lunch
Working time: about 25 minutes
Total time: about 1 hour and 10 minutes
(includes chilling)

Calories **110**	250 g	fresh spinach, stemmed and washed	8 oz
Protein **16g**	165 g	fresh sweetcorn kernels (from 1 large ear), or frozen sweetcorn kernels, thawed	5½ oz
Cholesterol **60mg**			
Total fat **3g**			
Saturated fat **0g**	500 g	white crab meat, picked over	1 lb
Sodium **240mg**	1	tomato, skinned, seeded and chopped	1
	2 tbsp	white wine vinegar	2 tbsp
	4 tbsp	creamy yogurt dressing (recipe, page 13)	4 tbsp
		cayenne pepper	
	⅛ tsp	salt	⅛ tsp
	1	red-leaf lettuce, washed and dried	1

Put the spinach, with just the water that clings to its leaves, into a pan. Cover the pan and steam the spinach over medium heat until it wilts — 2 to 3 minutes. Drain the spinach; when it is cool enough to handle, squeeze it to remove the excess liquid, and chop the spinach coarsely.

If you are using fresh sweetcorn, pour enough water

Calories **220**	350 g	white crab meat, picked over	12 oz
Protein **17g**	80 g	seedless green grapes, halved	2½ oz
Cholesterol **75mg**	80 g	seedless red grapes, halved	2½ oz
Total fat **8g**	1	bunch spring onions, white parts only, julienned	1
Saturated fat **1g**			
Sodium **225mg**	2	large oranges, juice only of 1	2
	¼ tsp	ground coriander	¼ tsp
	¼ tsp	ground cumin	¼ tsp
	¼ tsp	ground mace	¼ tsp
	¼ tsp	ground ginger	¼ tsp
	⅛ tsp	turmeric	⅛ tsp
	⅛ tsp	white pepper	⅛ tsp
	4 tbsp	mayonnaise (recipe, page 13)	4 tbsp
	250 g	celeriac, peeled and julienned	8 oz
	1	lemon, juice only	1
	1	lime, juice only	1
		freshly ground black pepper	
	6	kumquats (optional), sliced and seeded	6

In a large bowl, combine the crab meat, green and red grapes, spring onions and orange juice. In a small bowl, blend the coriander, cumin, mace, ginger, turmeric and white pepper into the mayonnaise; add this dressing to the crab meat salad and toss the ingredients well. Refrigerate the salad for at least 30 minutes.

Put the celeriac into a third bowl; sprinkle the celeriac with the lemon juice, lime juice and a generous grinding of black pepper. Toss the celeriac well and chill it for the same length of time as the salad.

Just before serving, segment the whole orange, cut away the peel, white pith and outer membrane, then

into a saucepan to fill it about 2.5 cm (1 inch) deep. Set a vegetable steamer in the pan and bring the water to the boil. Place the sweetcorn kernels in the steamer, cover the saucepan, and steam the sweetcorn until it is tender — about 4 minutes. (Thawed frozen sweetcorn requires no cooking.)

In a large bowl, combine the spinach, sweetcorn, crab meat, tomato and vinegar. Cover the bowl and refrigerate it for at least 30 minutes.

Shortly before assembling the salad, whisk together the yogurt dressing, a pinch of cayenne pepper and the salt. Pour the dressing over the salad and toss well. Arrange the lettuce leaves on a serving platter. Mound the salad on the leaves and serve immediately.

Squid Salad with Spring Onions and Coriander

Serves 4 as a main course
Working time: about 25 minutes
Total time: about 1 hour

Calories **175**
Protein **16g**
Cholesterol **223mg**
Total fat **8g**
Saturated fat **1g**
Sodium **400mg**

600 g	small squid, cleaned and skinned, tentacles reserved	1¼ lb
2 tbsp	virgin olive oil	2 tbsp
¼ tsp	salt	¼ tsp
	freshly ground black pepper	
1 tsp	coriander seeds, crushed	1 tsp
2 tbsp	sherry vinegar	2 tbsp
1 tbsp	fresh lemon juice	1 tbsp
½	sweet red pepper, seeded, deribbed and diced	½
½	sweet yellow pepper, seeded, deribbed and diced	½
4	spring onions, trimmed and sliced diagonally into thin ovals	4
1	large round lettuce, washed and dried	1
	lemon slices for garnish	

Slice the squid pouches into thin rings. Heat 1 tablespoon of the olive oil in a large, heavy frying pan over high heat. When the oil is hot, add the squid rings and tentacles, ⅛ teaspoon of the salt and some pepper. Sauté the squid, stirring constantly, until it turns opaque — about 2 minutes. Drain the squid well, reserving the cooking juices, and transfer the squid pieces to a large bowl; put the bowl in the refrigerator.

Pour the cooking juices into a small saucepan; add the crushed coriander and boil the liquid until only 2 tablespoons remain — about 3 minutes. Remove from the heat, then whisk in the vinegar, lemon juice, remaining salt and remaining oil. Pour this dressing over the squid; add the peppers and spring onions, and toss. Chill the salad for at least 30 minutes.

Just before serving the salad, grind in a generous amount of black pepper and toss well. Present the salad on the lettuce leaves, garnished with lemon slices.

Clam and Sweetcorn Salad

Serves 6 as a main course at lunch
Working time: about 45 minutes
Total time: about 1 hour and 15 minutes

Calories **150**
Protein **9g**
Cholesterol **25mg**
Total fat **8g**
Saturated fat **1g**
Sodium **100mg**

5	spring onions, trimmed and finely chopped	5
1	garlic clove, finely chopped	1
¼ litre	dry white wine	8 fl oz
4 tbsp	fresh lemon juice	4 tbsp
36	small hard-shell clams, scrubbed	36
250 g	mushrooms, wiped clean, stemmed and quartered	8 oz
3	carrots, cut diagonally into 5 mm (¼ inch) thick slices	3
3	sticks celery, trimmed and cut diagonally into 5 mm (¼ inch) thick slices	3
325 g	fresh sweetcorn kernels (from about 2 large ears), or frozen sweetcorn, thawed	11 oz
1 tbsp	chopped parsley	1 tbsp
1 tbsp	white wine vinegar	1 tbsp
	freshly ground black pepper	
2 tbsp	virgin olive oil	2 tbsp
500 g	fresh spinach, washed, stemmed and cut into chiffonade (page 51)	1 lb

Combine the spring onions, garlic, wine and 3 table-spoons of the lemon juice in a large pan. Bring the mixture to the boil. Add the clams to the boiling liquid. Cover the pan and cook the clams until they open — about 3 minutes. Using a slotted spoon, transfer the clams to a large bowl; discard any clams that remain closed. Strain the broth through a sieve lined with muslin into a bowl, taking care not to pour any of the accumulated sand into the sieve.

When the clams are cool enough to handle, remove them from their shells. Dip each clam into the broth to rinse off any residual sand. Transfer the rinsed clams to a bowl; cover the bowl and refrigerate it.

Strain the clam broth once more and pour it into a saucepan. Add the mushrooms and the remaining tablespoon of lemon juice to the saucepan. Bring the broth to the boil, then reduce the heat, cover the pan and simmer the mushrooms for 2 minutes. With a slotted spoon, transfer the mushrooms to a bowl.

Add the carrots and celery to the clam broth in the saucepan; cover the pan and simmer the vegetables for 3 minutes. Using a slotted spoon, add the carrots and celery to the mushrooms; do not discard the broth. Let the vegetables cool to room temperature.

If you are using fresh sweetcorn, pour enough water into a saucepan to fill it about 2.5 cm (1 inch) deep. Set a steamer in the saucepan and put the sweetcorn into the steamer. Bring the water to the boil, tightly cover the pan, and steam the sweetcorn for 3 minutes. (Frozen sweetcorn requires no steaming.)

To prepare the dressing, whisk the parsley, vinegar, some pepper and the oil into the reserved clam broth. Add all the vegetables to the bowl containing the clams; pour about three quarters of the dressing over the salad and toss it well.

Arrange the spinach chiffonade on individual plates. Spoon some of the salad on to each plate; pass the remaining dressing separately.

Mussel and Sprouted Lentil Salad

Serves 6 as a main course at lunch
Working time: about 35 minutes
Total time: about 1 hour (includes chilling)

Calories **120**
Protein **9g**
Cholesterol **25mg**
Total fat **4g**
Saturated fat **0g**
Sodium **225mg**

36	mussels, scrubbed and debearded	36
2	carrots, julienned	2
¼ tsp	salt	¼ tsp
	freshly ground black pepper	
2 tbsp	white wine vinegar	2 tbsp
1 tbsp	safflower oil	1 tbsp
1	garlic clove, finely chopped	1
500 g	ripe tomatoes, skinned, seeded, coarsely chopped, or 400 g (14 oz) canned tomatoes, drained, coarsely chopped	1 lb
1 tbsp	fennel seeds	1 tbsp
150 g	sprouted lentils (page 37)	5 oz
1	lettuce, washed and dried	1

Bring 12.5 cl (4 fl oz) of water to the boil in a large pan; add the mussels and cover the pan. Steam the mussels until they open — about 3 minutes. With a slotted spoon, remove the mussels and set them aside; discard any that remain closed. Strain the cooking liquid through a sieve lined with doubled muslin, taking care not to pour any of the sand into the sieve. Reserve the liquid.

When the mussels are cool enough to handle, re-

move them from their shells. Dip each mussel into the reserved liquid to rinse away any residual sand. Put the rinsed mussels into a large bowl. Reline the sieve with muslin and strain the liquid through it again; set the liquid aside.

Bring 1.5 litres (2½ pints) of water to the boil in a saucepan. Add the carrots and blanch them for 2 minutes, then refresh them under cold running water. Drain the carrots well, add them to the mussels, and season with the salt, some pepper and the vinegar.

Heat the oil in a heavy-bottomed saucepan over medium heat; add the garlic and sauté it for 1 minute. Add the tomatoes, the fennel seeds and 12.5 cl (4 fl oz) of the reserved mussel liquid; increase the heat to medium high and bring the liquid to the boil. Reduce the heat to maintain a strong simmer and cook the tomato mixture until nearly all the liquid has evaporated — about 5 minutes.

Meanwhile, blanch the lentil sprouts in 1.5 litres (2½ pints) of boiling water for 3 minutes. Drain them, refresh them under cold running water, and drain them again. Add the sprouts and the tomato mixture to the mussels and toss well. Refrigerate the salad for 1 hour before presenting it on a bed of lettuce.

Mussel Salad

Serves 4 as a first course
Working time: about 30 minutes
Total time: about 1 hour

Calories **175**
Protein **7g**
Cholesterol **25mg**
Total fat **5g**
Saturated fat **1g**
Sodium **125mg**

90 g	rice	3 oz
1 tbsp	fennel seeds	1 tbsp
2 tbsp	finely chopped sweet green pepper	2 tbsp
4 tbsp	finely chopped red onion	4 tbsp
1	small ripe tomato, skinned, seeded and chopped	1
1	small garlic clove, finely chopped	1
1 tbsp	grated horseradish, drained	1 tbsp
3 tbsp	white wine vinegar	3 tbsp
24	mussels, scrubbed and debearded	24
1 tbsp	virgin olive oil	1 tbsp
	parsley sprigs for garnish	

Put the rice, the fennel seeds and ¼ litre (8 fl oz) of water into a small saucepan over medium-high heat. Bring the water to the boil, then reduce the heat, cover the pan, and simmer the rice until it is tender — 20 to 25 minutes. Set the rice aside.

While the rice is simmering, prepare the marinade. In a non-reactive bowl, mix together the green pepper, onion, tomato, garlic, horseradish and vinegar. Set the marinade aside while you cook the mussels.

Bring ¼ litre (8 fl oz) of water to the boil in a large pan. Add the mussels and cover the pan. Steam the mussels until they open — 2 to 3 minutes. Discard any mussels that remain closed. Strain the cooking liquid through a sieve lined with doubled muslin, taking care not to pour any of the sand into the sieve. Reserve the liquid.

Using a slotted spoon, transfer the mussels to a large bowl. When the mussels are cool enough to handle, remove them from their shells, reserving one half of each shell. Dip each mussel into the reserved liquid to rinse away any residual sand. Pat the mussels dry, then add them to the marinade, and let them stand at room temperature for 30 minutes.

Stir the rice and oil into the marinated mussels. Fill each reserved mussel shell with one mussel and about 2 teaspoons of the rice-and-vegetable mixture. Arrange the stuffed shells on a platter; garnish the platter with the parsley just before serving.

Turkey Salad with Green and Red Grapes

Serves 4 as a main course
Working time: about 20 minutes
Total time: about 1 hour and 30 minutes

Calories **290**
Protein **27g**
Cholesterol **60mg**
Total fat **17g**
Saturated fat **2g**
Sodium **200mg**

500 g	skinless turkey breast meat	1 lb
2 tbsp	fresh lemon juice	2 tbsp
1 tbsp	virgin olive oil	1 tbsp
1 tbsp	fresh thyme, or 1 tsp dried thyme	1 tbsp
⅛ tsp	salt	⅛ tsp
	freshly ground black pepper	
2 tbsp	sliced almonds	2 tbsp
80 g	seedless green grapes	2½ oz
80 g	seedless red grapes	2½ oz
3	spring onions, trimmed and thinly sliced	3
4 tbsp	vinaigrette (recipe, page 13)	4 tbsp
1	small red-leaf lettuce, washed and dried	1

Preheat the oven to 190°C (375°F or Mark 5). Put the turkey meat in a small baking dish and sprinkle it with the lemon juice, oil, thyme, salt and some pepper. Rub the seasonings into the meat and let it marinate at room temperature for 20 minutes.

At the end of the marinating time, roast the meat, turning it once, until it feels firm but springy to the touch — about 20 minutes.

While the meat is cooking, spread the almonds on a small baking sheet and toast them in the oven until they are golden-brown — about 4 minutes. Set the toasted almonds aside.

When the turkey has finished cooking, remove it from the oven and let it cool in the dish. As soon as the meat is cool enough to handle, remove it from the dish and cut it diagonally into thin slices. Lay the slices in the pan juices and refrigerate them for at least 30 minutes.

To assemble the salad, combine the grapes, spring onions and vinaigrette in a bowl. Arrange the turkey slices on the lettuce leaves and mound the grapes and spring onions on top; sprinkle the salad with the toasted almonds and serve immediately.

Turkey and Peach Roses

Serves 6 as a main course
Working time: about 30 minutes
Total time: about 1 hour and 30 minutes

Calories **225**
Protein **27g**
Cholesterol **60mg**
Total fat **10g**
Saturated fat **2g**
Sodium **150mg**

1	skinned and boned turkey breast (about 750 g/1 ½ lb)	1
¼ tsp	salt	¼ tsp
3 tbsp	fresh orange juice	3 tbsp
1 ½ tbsp	red wine vinegar	1 ½ tbsp
¼ tsp	Dijon mustard	¼ tsp
	freshly ground black pepper	
1 ½ tbsp	safflower oil	1 ½ tbsp
1 ½ tbsp	virgin olive oil	1 ½ tbsp
3	large ripe peaches, fuzz wiped away with a cloth	3
1	red-leaf lettuce, washed and dried	1
3 tbsp	small basil or coriander leaves	3 tbsp

Sprinkle the turkey breast with ⅛ teaspoon of the salt. Enclose the breast tightly in doubled aluminium foil, creating a long waterproof package. Pour enough water into a large, deep saucepan to fill it about 7.5 cm (3 inches) deep. Bring the water to the barest simmer and add the breast. Cook the meat for 20 minutes, maintaining a simmer throughout the cooking; do not let the water come to the boil. Turn the turkey over and continue cooking it for 10 minutes more. Remove the turkey from the water and transfer it, still wrapped in foil, to the refrigerator.

To make the vinaigrette, combine the orange juice, vinegar, mustard, some pepper and the remaining salt in a small bowl. Whisking vigorously, pour in the safflower oil in a thin, steady stream; incorporate the olive oil the same way.

Cut the peaches in half, then cut each half into thin wedges; you will need 42 slices. Place the slices in a small bowl and spoon 3 tablespoons of the vinaigrette over them. Put the bowl in the refrigerator.

When the turkey breast is cool, remove the foil and cut the meat against the grain into 5 mm (¼ inch) thick slices; you will need 36 slices.

Line six salad plates with the lettuce leaves. To fashion the roses, first arrange three peach wedges in a loose circle on one of the plates. Place two larger turkey slices inside the circle, nestling them within the curve of the peaches and tucking their ends in. Next, arrange two peach wedges inside the circle, facing each other. Build another layer using two medium slices of turkey and two peach slices. To form the flower's centre, roll up a small turkey slice and insert it between the peaches; tightly roll up a final small slice of turkey and tuck it in the centre of the rose. Repeat the process to form five more roses from the remaining peach wedges and turkey slices. Dribble the remaining vinaigrette over the roses and garnish them with the basil or coriander leaves; serve immediately.

this marinade over the thighs, and stir to coat them. Cover the bowl and marinate the chicken for 2 hours in the refrigerator.

At the end of the marinating period, remove the thighs from the liquid and pat them dry with paper towels. Reserve the marinade. Heat the oil in a large, heavy saucepan over medium heat. Add the thighs and cook them until they are browned on all sides — about 10 minutes. Stir in the barley, the stock and 12.5 cl (4 fl oz) of the reserved marinade. Bring the liquid to the boil, reduce the heat, and simmer the mixture until the barley is tender and most of the liquid has evaporated — about 30 minutes.

Remove the thighs and set them aside; when they are cool enough to handle, pull the meat from the bones and chop it coarsely. Add the chicken to the barley, then add the parsley, the remaining mint and the remaining lemon juice. Mix the salad well and serve it on a bed of iceberg lettuce, garnished with the mint sprigs.

Chicken Salad with Barley and Mint

Serves 6 as a main course
Working time: about 45 minutes
Total time: about 3 hours and 20 minutes
(includes chilling)

Calories **410**
Protein **30g**
Cholesterol **80mg**
Total fat **15g**
Saturated fat **3g**
Sodium **320mg**

1 kg	chicken thighs, skinned and trimmed of fat	2 lb
15 cl	fresh lemon juice	¼ pint
½ tsp	ground cumin	½ tsp
½ tsp	dry mustard	½ tsp
½ tsp	paprika	½ tsp
½ tsp	ground cinnamon	½ tsp
½ tsp	cayenne pepper	½ tsp
½ tsp	salt	½ tsp
	freshly ground black pepper	
3 tbsp	chopped fresh mint, or 1 tbsp dried mint	3 tbsp
1	garlic clove, finely chopped	1
2 tbsp	safflower oil	2 tbsp
275 g	pearl barley	9 oz
1 litre	unsalted chicken stock	1¾ pints
1 tbsp	chopped parsley, preferably flat-leaf	1 tbsp
1	small iceberg lettuce, washed and dried	1
	several mint sprigs	

Put the chicken thighs in a large bowl. In a smaller bowl, combine 12.5 cl (4 fl oz) of the lemon juice, the cumin, mustard, paprika, cinnamon, cayenne pepper, salt, some black pepper, 1 tablespoon of the fresh mint or 1 teaspoon of dried mint, and the garlic. Pour

Chicken and Avocado Salad with Ricotta and Chives

Serves 4 as a main course
Working time: about 20 minutes
Total time: about 50 minutes

Calories **315**
Protein **40g**
Cholesterol **100 mg**
Total fat **17g**
Saturated fat **4g**
Sodium **265mg**

1 tsp	safflower oil	1 tsp
4	chicken breasts, skinned and boned (500 g/1 lb)	4
¼ tsp	salt	¼ tsp
	freshly ground black pepper	
250 g	low-fat ricotta cheese	8 oz
1 tbsp	low-fat plain yogurt	1 tbsp
2 tbsp	chopped chives	2 tbsp
1	spring onion, very finely sliced	1
1	head of radicchio or red-leaf lettuce, washed and dried	1
1	ripe avocado, stone removed, peeled, flesh rubbed with 1 tbsp fresh lemon juice	1
1	tomato, seeded and finely chopped (optional)	1
6	fresh basil leaves, thinly sliced (optional)	6

Heat the safflower oil in a large, heavy frying pan over very low heat. Sprinkle the chicken breasts with ⅛ teaspoon of the salt and some freshly ground pepper, and place them in the pan. Set a heavy plate on top of the chicken breasts to weight them down so that they will cook evenly. Cook the breasts on one side for 5 minutes; turn them over, again cover them with the plate, and cook them for 3 to 4 minutes more. The meat should feel firm but springy to the touch, with no traces of pink along the edges. Transfer the chicken breasts to a plate and refrigerate them while you prepare the rest of the salad.

Put the ricotta, yogurt, chopped chives and sliced spring onion into a bowl. Mix them well together, then cover the bowl and leave it to stand in a cool place for about 30 minutes.

Arrange a few radicchio or lettuce leaves on four plates. Slice the cooked chicken breasts diagonally and fan out each one of the leaves. Cut the peeled avocado into thin slices and tuck the slices between the chicken slices, then spoon a neat mound of the ricotta mixture on to the base of each chicken fan. If using, sprinkle the chopped tomato and basil over the top and, if you like, a little freshly ground pepper.

EDITOR'S NOTE: *Because avocado darkens when exposed to air, it should be rubbed generously with lemon juice immediately after peeling.*

Curried Chicken Salad with Raisins

Serves 6 as a main course
Working time: about 20 minutes
Total time: about 1 hour

Calories **250**
Protein **20g**
Cholesterol **55mg**
Total fat **9g**
Saturated fat **2g**
Sodium **190mg**

1 tsp	safflower oil	1 tsp
6	chicken breasts, skinned and boned (about 750 g/1 ½ lb)	6
¼ tsp	salt	¼ tsp
75 g	raisins	2 ½ oz
1	large carrot, grated	1
1	onion, grated	1
1	stick celery, chopped	1
3 tbsp	fresh lemon juice	3 tbsp
1 tbsp	curry powder	1 tbsp
1 tbsp	honey	1 tbsp
4 tbsp	mayonnaise (recipe, page 13)	4 tbsp
100 g	radishes, julienned	3 ½ oz
½ tbsp	virgin olive oil	½ tbsp
1	small cos lettuce, washed and dried	1
2	ripe tomatoes, cut into wedges	2

Heat the safflower oil in a large, heavy frying pan over low heat. Sprinkle the chicken breasts with the salt and place them in the pan. Set a heavy plate on top of the chicken breasts to weight them down so that they will cook evenly. Cook the breasts on the first side for 5 minutes; turn them over, weight them down again with the plate, and cook them on the second side for 3 to 4 minutes. The meat should feel firm but springy to the touch, with no traces of pink along the edges. Transfer the breasts to a plate and allow them to cool. When the chicken is cool enough to handle, cut it into 2.5 cm (1 inch) cubes.

In a large mixing bowl, toss the chicken cubes with the raisins, grated carrot and onion, chopped celery, lemon juice, curry powder, honey and mayonnaise. Chill the salad for at least 30 minutes.

Toss the radish julienne with the olive oil in a small bowl. Mound the chicken salad on the lettuce leaves, and garnish each plate with the radish julienne and the tomato wedges. Serve immediately.

Salad of Grilled Quail with Dried Fruits

Serves 4 as a main course
Working time: about 45 minutes
Total time: about 2 hours and 30 minutes
(includes marinating)

Calories **480**
Protein **25g**
Cholesterol **85mg**
Total fat **22g**
Saturated fat **4g**
Sodium **300mg**

4	quail	4
2	spring onions, trimmed and finely chopped	2
2	garlic cloves, finely chopped	2
2 tbsp	safflower oil	2 tbsp
6 tbsp	Armagnac or brandy	6 tbsp
¼ tsp	salt	¼ tsp
1 tsp	fresh thyme, or ¼ tsp dried thyme	1 tsp
1 tsp	chili powder	1 tsp
45 g	sultanas	1½ oz
45 g	raisins	1½ oz
45 g	currants	1½ oz
45 g	dried apricots, sliced	1½ oz
2 tbsp	sugar	2 tbsp
1 tbsp	grated orange rind	1 tbsp
¼ litre	unsalted chicken stock	8 fl oz
4 tbsp	fresh lemon juice	4 tbsp
1 tbsp	grainy mustard	1 tbsp
250 g	fresh spinach, washed, stemmed, dried	8 oz
30 g	fresh sorrel (optional), washed, stemmed and dried	1 oz

Lay a quail breast side down on a cutting board. To halve the bird, cut through the back, from neck to tail, along one side of the backbone. Spread the quail open and cut through the centre of the breastbone from neck to tail. Halve the remaining quail the same way. Put the quail halves into a baking dish large enough to accommodate them in a single layer.

Whisk together the spring onions, garlic, 1 table-spoon of the oil, 2 tablespoons of the Armagnac or brandy, the salt, thyme and chili powder. Pour this marinade over the quail halves and turn them once or twice in the liquid to coat them evenly. Cover the dish and refrigerate it for 2 hours.

About half way through the marinating period, pre-pare the dried fruits. Put the sultanas, raisins, currants, apricots, sugar and orange rind into a saucepan. Pour in enough water to cover the fruits by about 1 cm (½ inch). Bring to the boil, then reduce the heat and sim-mer for 5 minutes. Pour in the stock, the lemon juice, and the remaining Armagnac or brandy, and simmer until reduced by half — about 40 minutes. Strain the fruits, reserving their cooking liquid.

When the quail finish marinating, grill them in their baking dish for 5 to 7 minutes per side. While the quail are cooking, put the spinach and the sorrel, if you are using it, into a large bowl. In a small bowl, whisk together the reserved cooking liquid, the remaining tablespoon of oil and the mustard. Pour half of this dressing over the greens and toss well.

Arrange the dressed greens on individual plates and top them with the fruits. Set two quail halves on each plate; pour the remaining dressing over all and serve.

Chicken and Grapefruit Salad

Serves 6 as a main course
Working time: about 1 hour and 15 minutes
Total time: about 3 hours and 30 minutes
(includes marinating)

Calories **350**
Protein **26g**
Cholesterol **80mg**
Total fat **13g**
Saturated fat **3g**
Sodium **300mg**

1 kg	chicken thighs, skinned, trimmed of fat	2 lb
15 cl	dry vermouth	¼ pint
½ tsp	salt	½ tsp
1 tbsp	chopped fresh oregano, or 1 tsp dried oregano	1 tbsp
1 tsp	aniseeds	1 tsp
2	garlic cloves, finely chopped	2
1	shallot, finely chopped	1
3 tbsp	honey	3 tbsp
	freshly ground black pepper	
2 tbsp	virgin olive oil	2 tbsp
4	carrots, quartered lengthwise and cut into 2.5 cm (1 inch) lengths	4
4	sticks celery, halved lengthwise and cut into 2.5 cm (1 inch) lengths	4
12.5 cl	unsalted chicken stock	4 fl oz
4	grapefruits	4
1	bunch watercress, trimmed, washed and dried	1

Put the chicken thighs into a bowl with the vermouth, salt, oregano, aniseeds, garlic, shallot, 2 tablespoons of the honey and some pepper. Stir to combine the ingredients, then cover the bowl and let the chicken marinate in the refrigerator for 2 hours.

At the end of the marinating period, preheat the oven to 190°C (375°F or Mark 5). Drain the chicken and pat it dry with paper towels. Strain the marinade, reserving both liquid and solids. Heat the oil in a heavy fireproof casserole over medium-high heat. Add the chicken thighs to the casserole and sauté them until they are browned on all sides — about 10 minutes. Remove the thighs from the casserole. Add the reserved solids and sauté them for 1 minute. Add the carrots and celery, then pour in the stock, and simmer the mixture for 2 minutes.

Set the chicken thighs on top of the vegetables in the casserole and transfer the casserole, uncovered, to the oven. Bake the chicken and vegetables, stirring occasionally, until the juices run clear from a thigh pierced with a knife — about 25 minutes.

Remove the chicken from the casserole and set it aside to cool. Then remove the vegetables and set them aside to cool as well.

While the chicken and vegetables are cooling, prepare the grapefruits and the dressing. Cut away the peel and pith from a grapefruit. To separate the segments from the inner membranes, slice down to the core on either side of each segment, working over a bowl to catch the juice. Discard the seeds and set the segments aside as you go. Squeeze the pulpy core of membranes over the bowl to extract every bit of juice. Repeat the process to segment the remaining three grapefruits.

Pour the reserved marinade into a small saucepan. Add the grapefruit juice and the remaining honey. Bring the liquid to the boil and cook it until it is reduced to about 15 cl (¼ pint) — 5 to 10 minutes.

When the chicken is cool enough to handle, pull the meat from the bones and cut it into thin strips. Arrange the watercress on a platter. Top it with the vegetables, then with a layer of the grapefruit segments. Scatter the chicken on top of the grapefruit; just before serving the salad, pour the reduced marinade over all.

Lamb Salad with Fig Sauce

Serves 8 as a main course
Working time: about 35 minutes
Total time: about 2 hours

Calories **385**
Protein **24g**
Cholesterol **60mg**
Total fat **22g**
Saturated fat **10g**
Sodium **155mg**

1 tbsp	safflower oil	1 tbsp
1.5 kg	leg of lamb shank end, trimmed of fat	3 lb
¼ tsp	salt	¼ tsp
	freshly ground black pepper	
2 tbsp	virgin olive oil	2 tbsp
175 g	dried figs, quartered	6 oz
4 tbsp	chopped shallot	4 tbsp
½ tbsp	fresh thyme, or ½ tsp dried thyme	½ tbsp
¼ litre	unsalted veal or chicken stock	8 fl oz
5 tbsp	sherry vinegar or red wine vinegar	5 tbsp
1	large Batavian endive (about 750 g/1 ½ lb), washed and dried	1
	several thyme sprigs for garnish (optional)	

Preheat the oven to 180°C (350°F or Mark 4). Heat the safflower oil in a large shallow fireproof casserole over medium-high heat. Add the lamb and brown it well on all sides — 10 to 12 minutes. Sprinkle the lamb with the salt and some pepper, then transfer the casserole to the oven. If you like your meat medium rare, roast the lamb for about 1 hour; if you prefer it medium, roast the lamb for 1¼ hours. Remove the lamb from the casserole and set it aside to cool.

Return the casserole to the stove, setting it over medium heat. Add 1 tablespoon of the olive oil, the figs, shallot, thyme and some pepper. Cook the mixture, stirring frequently, for 3 minutes. Pour in the stock and 4 tablespoons of the vinegar. Reduce the heat to low and simmer the mixture, stirring occasionally, for 5 minutes.

Remove 16 fig quarters from the casserole and set them aside. To make the sauce, transfer the remaining contents of the casserole to a food processor or a blender. Purée the mixture, scraping down the sides at least once during the process. Transfer the sauce to a bowl and chill it.

When the lamb has cooled, slice it thinly against the grain. Toss the Batavian endive with the remaining olive oil, the remaining vinegar and a generous grinding of black pepper.

Spread the endive on individual salad plates and arrange the lamb slices on top. Pour the fig sauce over the lamb; garnish the salads with the reserved fig quarters and the thyme sprigs, and serve immediately.

Lamb Salad with Marinated Aubergine

Serves 6 as a main course
Working time: about 50 minutes
Total time: about 3 hours (includes marinating)

Calories **305**
Protein **23g**
Cholesterol **55mg**
Total fat **18g**
Saturated fat **9g**
Sodium **155mg**

750 g	boneless leg of lamb, trimmed of fat	1½ lb
1½ tsp	chopped fresh rosemary, or ½ tsp dried rosemary, crumbled	1½ tsp
1	small red onion, chopped	1
	freshly ground black pepper	
3 tbsp	red wine	3 tbsp
3 tbsp	red wine vinegar	3 tbsp
1	aubergine (about 500 g/1 lb), quartered lengthwise and thinly sliced	1
½ tsp	salt	½ tsp
1 tbsp	fresh thyme, or 1 tsp dried thyme	1 tbsp
1 tsp	chopped parsley	1 tsp
1 tbsp	olive oil	1 tbsp
2 tbsp	balsamic vinegar, or 1½ tbsp red wine vinegar mixed with ½ tsp honey	2 tbsp
3 tbsp	tomato paste	3 tbsp
500 g	ripe tomatoes, skinned, seeded and chopped	1 lb
1	bunch watercress, washed, stemmed and dried	1

Lay the leg of lamb in a shallow, non-reactive dish. Scatter the rosemary and onion over the meat, then season it with some pepper, and pour in the wine and wine vinegar. Turn the meat to moisten both sides. Cover the dish and marinate the lamb in the refrigerator for 2 hours.

Toss the aubergine slices with the salt and drain them in a colander for 1 hour.

Preheat the oven to 230°C (450°F or Mark 8). Rinse the aubergine slices and pat them dry, then transfer them to a roasting pan. Sprinkle the thyme and parsley over the slices; dribble the oil over the top. Bake the aubergine slices, stirring frequently, until they are tender — about 25 minutes.

Transfer the aubergine slices to a bowl. Whisk together the balsamic vinegar or wine vinegar mixed with honey, and 2 tablespoons of the tomato paste. Pour this mixture over the aubergine slices, mix well and set the bowl aside.

Remove the lamb and pat it dry. Reserve the marinade for the dressing. Put the lamb in a roasting pan and roast it until it is medium rare — about 1 hour. Transfer the lamb to a cutting board and let it rest.

To make the dressing, pour the reserved marinade into the roasting pan. Set the pan on the stove and bring the liquid to the boil, scraping with a wooden spoon to dissolve the pan deposits. Strain the liquid into a small bowl, then stir in the chopped tomatoes and the remaining tomato paste; set the dressing aside.

Slice the lamb and arrange it on a platter with the watercress and the aubergine. Pour some of the dressing over the lamb and present the rest alongside.

Pork, Nectarine and Orange Salad

Serves 4 as a main course
Working time: about 40 minutes
Total time: about 1 hour and 10 minutes

Calories **310**
Protein **27g**
Cholesterol **80mg**
Total fat **12g**
Saturated fat **2g**
Sodium **250mg**

½ tsp	ground ginger	½ tsp
½ tsp	dry mustard	½ tsp
½ tsp	ground coriander	½ tsp
¼ tsp	cayenne pepper	¼ tsp
¼ tsp	salt	¼ tsp
500 g	pork fillet, trimmed of fat	1 lb
2 tbsp	safflower oil	2 tbsp
3	navel oranges	3
3 tbsp	sherry vinegar	3 tbsp
1 tbsp	chopped fresh coriander	1 tbsp
3	nectarines, cut into wedges	3
1	bunch young beet greens, or 125 g (4 oz) spinach, washed, stemmed and dried	1

Preheat the oven to 200°C (400°F or Mark 6).

Combine the ginger, mustard, coriander, cayenne pepper and salt in a small bowl. Rub this mixture into the pork fillet with your hands.

Heat ½ tablespoon of the oil in a large, shallow fireproof casserole over medium-high heat. Add the pork and sauté it until it is well browned on all sides — 5 to 6 minutes. Transfer the casserole to the oven and roast the pork until it feels firm to the touch and the juices run clear when it is pierced with a skewer — 20 to 25 minutes. Remove the pork from the casserole and cool to room temperature — about 20 minutes.

While the pork is roasting, prepare the oranges. First cut away the peel and the white pith below it. Then, to separate the orange segments from the internal membranes, slice down to the core on either side of each segment, holding the fruit over a bowl to catch the juice. Set the segments aside as you go.

Drain off any fat in the casserole and return the pan to the stove over medium-high heat. Pour in the vinegar and the orange juice; bring the liquid to the boil, scraping constantly with a wooden spoon to dissolve any caramelized juices. Strain the liquid into a large bowl; whisk in the coriander and the remaining oil, then add the orange and nectarine pieces, and toss the mixture well.

With a slotted spoon, transfer the fruit to a plate lined with the beet greens or spinach. Slice the pork thinly and arrange the slices with the fruit. Pour the dressing remaining in the bowl over all. Serve at once.

Pork and Clam Salad

Serves 6 as a main course
Working time: about 1 hour and 30 minutes
Total time: about 3 hours and 15 minutes
(includes chilling)

Calories **425**
Protein **27g**
Cholesterol **75mg**
Total fat **9g**
Saturated fat **2g**
Sodium **290mg**

500 g	boneless pork loin, trimmed of fat and cut into 1 cm (½ inch) cubes	1 lb
¼ litre	dry white wine	8 fl oz
2 tbsp	fresh lemon juice	2 tbsp
½ tsp	salt	½ tsp
	freshly ground black pepper	
¼ tsp	cayenne pepper	¼ tsp
2 tbsp	chopped fresh coriander	2 tbsp
4	garlic cloves, finely chopped	4
2 tbsp	virgin olive oil	2 tbsp
1	shallot, finely chopped	1
36	small hard-shell clams, scrubbed	36
1	small red onion, thinly sliced	1
1	small sweet red pepper, seeded, deribbed and cut into short, thin strips	1
1	small sweet green pepper, seeded, deribbed and cut into short, thin strips	1
4	ripe tomatoes, skinned, seeded and julienned	4
275 g	long-grain rice	9 oz
½ litre	unsalted chicken stock	16 fl oz
1	bunch watercress, trimmed, washed and dried	1

Combine the pork, wine, 1 tablespoon of the lemon juice, the salt, some black pepper, the cayenne pepper, 1 tablespoon of the coriander and half of the chopped garlic in a non-reactive bowl. Cover the bowl and refrigerate it for 2 hours.

Heat 1 tablespoon of the olive oil in a large pan over medium-high heat. Add the shallot and the remaining garlic, and sauté them for 1 minute. Put the clams into the pan. Cover the pan and cook the clams, stirring occasionally, until they open — 3 to 5 minutes. Using a slotted spoon, transfer the clams to a large bowl; discard any clams that remain closed. Strain the cooking liquid through a sieve lined with muslin, taking care not to pour into the sieve any of the accumulated sand from the pan. Discard the solids.

When the clams are cool enough to handle, remove them from their shells, then dip them one at a time into the strained cooking liquid to rinse off any residual grains of sand. Transfer the rinsed clams to a bowl. Rinse out the muslin and reline the sieve with it. Strain the broth again and pour it over the clams.   ▶

Add to the clams the remaining lemon juice, the onion, red pepper, green pepper, tomatoes and the remaining coriander; toss the mixture well, then cover the bowl and refrigerate it.

Remove the pork loin cubes from the marinade, reserving the marinade; pat the meat dry. Heat the remaining tablespoon of oil in a heavy saucepan over medium-high heat. Add the pork cubes and sauté them until they are browned — about 5 minutes.

Add the rice, stock and reserved marinade to the pan. Bring the liquid to the boil, then reduce the heat and simmer the mixture, covered, until the rice has absorbed all the liquid and is tender — 18 to 20 minutes. Remove the pork and rice from the pan and spread it in a flat dish; when it is cool, mix it with the clams and vegetables. Serve the salad on a bed of watercress.

Shredded Beef Salad with Marinated Carrot Strips

Serves 8 as a main course
Working time: about 45 minutes
Total time: about 4 hours

Calories **255**
Protein **27g**
Cholesterol **75mg**
Total fat **12g**
Saturated fat **4g**
Sodium **190mg**

3 tbsp	safflower oil	3 tbsp
1 kg	lean beef chuck, or other braising steak, trimmed of fat	2 lb
6	medium carrots	6
¼ litre	unsalted veal or chicken stock	8 fl oz
2	onions, coarsely chopped	2
3	garlic cloves, crushed	3
1 tbsp	fresh thyme, or 1 tsp dried thyme	1 tbsp
3	bay leaves	3
1 tsp	sugar	1 tsp
12.5 cl	cider vinegar	4 fl oz
¼ tsp	salt	¼ tsp
2 tbsp	hoisin sauce	2 tbsp
	freshly ground black pepper	
	several Chinese cabbage or Batavian endive leaves, washed and dried	
4	spring onions (optional), cut into brushes and soaked in iced water	4

Heat 1 tablespoon of the safflower oil in a large, heavy sauté pan over medium-high heat. Add the beef and sear it in the oil until it is well browned on all sides — about 10 minutes.

Slice one of the carrots into thin rounds and add it to the pan along with the stock, onions, garlic, thyme and bay leaves. Pour in enough water to raise the depth of the liquid in the pan to about 2.5 cm (1 inch). Bring the liquid to a simmer, then reduce the heat to low; partially cover the pan and cook the beef slowly until it is quite tender — about 3 hours. If the liquid falls below 5 mm (¼ inch) during the cooking, add another 12.5 cl (4 fl oz) of water to the pan.

While the meat is cooking, use a vegetable peeler to pare long, thin strips from the outside of the remaining five carrots; discard the woody cores. Put the strips into a large bowl with the sugar and all but 2 tablespoons of the vinegar; toss well. Set the carrot strips aside to marinate, stirring them from time to time.

When the beef is tender, remove it from the pan and set it aside. Strain the cooking liquid; pour half of it into a small saucepan and discard the rest. Rapidly boil the liquid until only 4 tablespoons remain. Skim any fat from the surface and set the liquid aside.

When the beef is cool enough to handle, shred it with your fingers, discarding any fat. Heat 1 tablespoon of the remaining oil in the pan over medium-high heat. Add the beef and the salt; sauté the beef, stirring constantly, for 1 minute. Pour in the reduced cooking liquid, the remaining vinegar and the hoisin sauce; sprinkle in some pepper and cook the beef for 1 minute more, stirring all the while. Transfer the beef to a bowl and chill it.

Rinse out and dry the sauté pan, then return it to the stove over medium-high heat. Pour in the remaining oil; when it is hot, add the carrot strips and their marinade. Sauté the strips, stirring constantly, until all the liquid has evaporated — 1 to 2 minutes. Transfer the carrot strips to a bowl and chill them for 30 minutes.

To serve the salad, arrange the Chinese cabbage or Batavian endive leaves on a large plate; scatter the carrot strips on top, mound the beef in the centre and garnish with the spring onions if you are using them.

Pot-au-Feu Salad

Serves 4 as a main course
Working time: about 50 minutes
Total time: about 5 hours and 30 minutes
(includes chilling)

Calories **510**
Protein **33g**
Cholesterol **100mg**
Total fat **23g**
Saturated fat **5g**
Sodium **400mg**

½ tbsp	safflower oil	½ tbsp
500 g	beef topside, trimmed of fat	1 lb
1	calf's foot or 2 pig's trotters	1
¼ tsp	salt	¼ tsp
2 litres	unsalted veal or chicken stock	3½ pints
4	carrots, cut into 5 cm (2 inch) segments, each segment quartered lengthwise	4
2	turnips, peeled, each cut into wedges	2
4	leeks, trimmed, split lengthwise and washed thoroughly to remove all grit	4
4	small round red potatoes, each cut into wedges	4
2 tbsp	chopped parsley	2 tbsp
1	lettuce, washed and dried	1
12.5 cl	mayonnaise (recipe, page 13)	4 fl oz

Heat the safflower oil in a large, heavy saucepan over medium-high heat. Add the beef and brown it on all sides — about 10 minutes. Next add the calf's foot or pig's trotters, the salt and the stock; bring the liquid to a simmer and cook it for 1½ hours. Strain and reserve the broth. Reserve the beef; discard the other solids.

Rinse out the pan and return the beef and broth to it. Add the carrots, turnips, leeks and potatoes, and bring the liquid to the boil. Reduce the heat to low and simmer the pot-au-feu until all the ingredients are tender — about 35 minutes. Remove the pan from the heat and let the contents cool to room temperature — about 30 minutes. Spoon the fat from the surface, then blot any remaining traces with a paper towel. Remove the beef and vegetables from the broth and set them aside in the refrigerator. Pour ½ litre (16 fl oz) of the broth into a bowl and stir the parsley into it, then divide the broth among four ramekins; chill the ramekins until the broth has set — about 2 hours.

Slice the beef and arrange it with the vegetables on individual lettuce-lined plates. Briefly dip the bottom of a ramekin into hot water; invert the ramekin on to one of the plates to release the jellied broth, then lift away the mould. Unmould the other ramekins in the same way. Serve the salads with the mayonnaise alongside.

Beef and Apple Salad with Stilton Cheese Dressing

Serves 4 as a main course
Working time: about 40 minutes
Total time: about 1 hour and 20 minutes

Calories **340**
Protein **28g**
Cholesterol **90mg**
Total fat **16g**
Saturated fat **6g**
Sodium **515mg**

400 g	thick piece of beef rump or sirloin steak	14 oz
1 tbsp	cracked black peppercorns	1 tbsp
12.5 cl	stout or dark beer	4 fl oz
4 tbsp	grated fresh horseradish, or 2 tbsp prepared horseradish, drained	4 tbsp
100 g	shallot, finely chopped	3½ oz
120 g	celery, chopped	4 oz
2	tart green apples, peeled, cored and cut into small pieces	2
2 tbsp	cut fresh chives	2 tbsp
1	bunch watercress, washed and dried	1
3½ tbsp	mayonnaise (recipe, page 13)	3½ tbsp
60 g	Stilton cheese, crumbled	2 oz
1	lemon, juice only	1
¼ tsp	salt	¼ tsp

Preheat the oven to 230°C (450°F or Mark 8). Rub the beef with the cracked pepper, pressing the grains into the meat with the palm of your hand. Heat a shallow fireproof casserole over medium-high heat. Set the beef in the pan with its fat side down; briefly sear the beef to render some of the fat. When a thin layer of fat covers the bottom of the pan, turn the beef over and brown it on the other side. Continue turning the beef until it is browned all over — about 5 minutes.

Transfer the casserole to the oven and roast the beef for 10 minutes. Remove the casserole and pour 4 tablespoons of the stout or beer over the roast. Return the roast to the oven and cook it until it is medium rare — about 20 minutes more. Remove the roast from the casserole and set it aside to cool.

Pour the remaining stout or beer into the casserole and set it over medium-high heat. Simmer the liquid, scraping the bottom of the pan with a wooden spoon until any caramelized juices have dissolved — about 2 minutes. Pour the liquid into a small heatproof bowl; set the bowl in the freezer for about 30 minutes.

While the liquid is chilling, assemble the rest of the salad. Trim the roast of fat and cut the beef into julienne. Transfer the beef to a large bowl and add the horseradish, shallot, celery, apples and chives. Pluck the leaves from half of the watercress stems and add the leaves to the mixture.

To make the dressing, lift the layer of congealed fat from the surface of the chilled liquid. Whisk the liquid with the mayonnaise, cheese, lemon juice and salt. Pour the dressing over the contents of the bowl and toss the salad well. Present the salad on a serving platter, garnished with the remaining watercress.

4 Microwaved scallops and slices of courgette nestle in a wreath of shredded radicchio (recipe, opposite). The salad is dressed with a ginger vinaigrette.

Surprising Paths to Freshness

Unexpected refinements in the salad-maker's art can be achieved with a microwave oven. The microwave allows a multitude of salad ingredients to be prepared with a fine touch, be they vegetables, seafood or fowl. And whether the intended effect is simple or sophisticated, the preparation and assembly of a salad are accomplished in a short space of time: for the nine recipes that follow, the working time averages just a little over 20 minutes.

Chief among the microwave's qualifications for salad-making is the gentle treatment it accords all manner of fresh vegetables, from the asparagus for moulded timbales on page 136 to the courgettes, mushrooms and red pepper that make up the vegetable salad à la Grecque on page 133. Thanks to their abbreviated cooking time and the little water needed to cook them, these vegetables emerge from the oven with their nutrients, texture and brilliant colour intact. By the same token, traditionally slow-cooking root vegetables may be quickly prepared to form the base of a salad: in the recipes in this section, beetroots are microwaved for 6 to 8 minutes, potatoes for 12 to 14.

Even the mainstays of fish and shellfish salads can be handled — with care — in the microwave. In Salade Niçoise *(page 130)*, thinly sliced fresh tuna is poached for several minutes in a dressing of tarragon, Dijon mustard and stock taken piping hot from the microwave oven; the tuna is then tossed with other elements of the salad and chilled before serving. Scallops, too, are ideally suited for the microwave process; to the benefit of the chilled main course salad in which they are highlighted *(right)*, the scallops retain their full measure of moisture and flavour.

Not to be overlooked is the microwave's versatility when it comes to preparing salad dressings. In some cases, the microwave produces a dressing that is poured over the salad while the liquid is still hot. The potato salad on page 132, for example, features a hot dressing based on celery, red onion and bacon, while the key to creating the wilted spinach salad on page 135 is a hot dressing of rice vinegar, sugar, soy sauce and pearl onions.

Because power settings often vary among different manufacturers' ovens, the recipes use "high" to indicate 100 per cent power, "medium high" for 70 per cent and "medium low" for 30 per cent.

Scallop and Courgette Salad on a Bed of Radicchio

Serves 4 as a main course at lunch
Working time: about 15 minutes
Total time: about 40 minutes

Calories **120**
Protein **15g**
Cholesterol **30mg**
Total fat **4g**
Saturated fat **1g**
Sodium **210mg**

350 g	scallops, rinsed, the bright white connective tissue removed	12 oz
1	small courgette (about 125 g/4 oz), trimmed and cut into paper-thin slices	1
2 tbsp	thinly sliced crystallized ginger	2 tbsp
2½ tbsp	fresh lemon juice	2½ tbsp
¼ tsp	salt	¼ tsp
	freshly ground black pepper	
1 tbsp	virgin olive oil	1 tbsp
1	head of radicchio or red-leaf lettuce (about 125 g/4 oz), washed, dried and cut into chiffonade (page 51)	1

Slice the scallops into very thin rounds. In a shallow glass bowl, combine the scallops with the courgette, 1½ tablespoons of the ginger, 1½ tablespoons of the lemon juice, the salt and some pepper. Set the bowl aside for 5 minutes; stir the contents and allow them to stand for 5 minutes more.

Microwave the scallops and courgette in their marinade for 2 to 3 minutes on high, stirring midway through the cooking.

Put the remaining ½ tablespoon of ginger in a small bowl. Set a strainer over the bowl and pour the scallop mixture into the strainer. Refrigerate both strainer and bowl for at least 15 minutes.

At the end of the chilling time, whisk the remaining tablespoon of lemon juice, the oil and more pepper into the marinade; then stir in the scallop mixture. Arrange the chiffonade in the shape of a wreath on a plate. Mound the salad in the centre and serve at once.

Salade Niçoise

Serves 4 as a main course
Working time: about 30 minutes
Total time: about 1 hour and 45 minutes
(includes chilling)

Calories **380**
Protein **35g**
Cholesterol **45mg**
Total fat **13g**
Saturated fat **2g**
Sodium **210mg**

500 g	small round red potatoes	1 lb
250 g	French beans, trimmed	8 oz
3	oil-cured black olives, stoned and coarsely chopped	3
250 g	ripe tomatoes, cored and cut into 1 cm (½ inch) thick slices	8 oz
2	hard-boiled eggs, the yolks discarded, the whites coarsely chopped	2
2 tbsp	white wine vinegar	2 tbsp
2 tbsp	chopped fresh tarragon, or 2 tsp dried tarragon	2 tbsp
2 tsp	Dijon mustard	2 tsp
1	small red onion, peeled, sliced and separated into rings	1
1	garlic clove, finely chopped	1
6 tbsp	fish stock or unsalted chicken stock	6 tbsp
	freshly ground black pepper	
500 g	raw tuna fillet, cut into 1 cm (½ inch) wide strips	1 lb
1 tbsp	virgin olive oil	1 tbsp
2	round lettuces, washed and dried	2

Prick the potatoes with a fork in two places; any more punctures would let too much moisture escape. Arrange them in a circle on absorbent paper towel in the microwave oven and cook them on high for 4 minutes. Turn the potatoes over and rearrange them in the oven; continue cooking them until they are barely tender —3 to 4 minutes more. Set them aside to cool.

While the potatoes are cooling, cook the beans: put them in a bowl and pour in 4 tablespoons of water. Cover the bowl and microwave on high until the beans are tender but still crisp — 3 to 4 minutes. Drain the beans and refresh them under cold running water, then drain them again and transfer them to a salad bowl. Peel the potatoes and cut them into 2.5 cm (1 inch) chunks. Add the potatoes, olives, tomatoes and egg whites to the beans.

Dry the bowl in which you cooked the beans and combine the vinegar, tarragon, mustard, onion, garlic, stock and some pepper in it. Cook the mixture on high until it comes to the boil — about 3 minutes. Remove the bowl from the oven. Rinse the tuna, pat it dry, and add it to the bowl. Stir the contents to distribute the tuna, then cover the bowl tightly, and set it aside for 3 minutes. The tuna should be opaque and firm to the touch; if it is not, drain the liquid into another bowl, reheat it, and pour it over the tuna strips for a second 3 minute steeping.

Add the cooked tuna and its steeping liquid to the bowl containing the beans. Pour in the oil and toss the ingredients gently. Refrigerate the salad for at least 45 minutes before serving it on a bed of lettuce leaves.

Julienned Beetroots with Dijon Mustard

Serves 4 as a first course
Working time: about 15 minutes
Total time: about 30 minutes

Calories **70**	3	beetroots, of equal size (about 350 g/12 oz)	3
Protein **1g**	1	shallot, finely chopped	1
Cholesterol **0mg**	1½ tbsp	Dijon mustard	1½ tbsp
Total fat **4g**	1½ tbsp	red wine vinegar	1½ tbsp
Saturated fat **0g**		freshly ground black pepper	
Sodium **115mg**	1 tbsp	virgin olive oil	1 tbsp
	1	round lettuce (about 125 g/4 oz), washed and dried	1

Rinse the beetroots but do not pat them dry. Put them on a plate and microwave them on high for 6 to 8 minutes, turning them over about half way through the cooking time. Remove them from the oven, wrap them in a large piece of aluminium foil, and let them stand for 15 minutes to complete their cooking.

In a small bowl, combine the shallot, mustard, vinegar, some pepper and 1 tablespoon of water. Whisk in the oil and set the vinaigrette aside.

Peel and julienne the beetroots. Combine the julienne with about three quarters of the vinaigrette; toss well and refrigerate until cool.

Just before serving, slice the lettuce into chiffonade (page 51) and toss it with the remaining vinaigrette. Divide the lettuce evenly among four salad plates, top with the beetroot julienne, and serve at once.

Bacon and Onion Potato Salad

Serves 6 as a side dish
Working time: about 10 minutes
Total time: about 20 minutes

Calories **140**
Protein **3g**
Cholesterol **2mg**
Total fat **2g**
Saturated fat **0g**
Sodium **45mg**

1 kg	small round red potatoes of equal size, scrubbed	2 lb
2	rashers bacon, cut into thin strips	2
40 g	red onion, thinly sliced	1½ oz
4 tbsp	finely chopped celery	4 tbsp
1 tbsp	cornflour, mixed with 12.5 cl (4 fl oz) unsalted chicken stock	1 tbsp
4 tbsp	white vinegar	4 tbsp
	freshly ground black pepper	
2 tbsp	coarsely chopped parsley	2 tbsp

Prick the potatoes with a fork in two places; any more punctures would let too much moisture escape.

Arrange them in a circle on absorbent paper towel in the microwave oven; cook them on high for 7 minutes. Turn the potatoes over and rearrange them; continue cooking them on high until they are barely soft — 5 to 7 minutes more. Remove the potatoes from the oven and set them aside until they are cool enough to handle.

Put the bacon strips in a bowl; cover the bowl with a paper towel and microwave the bacon on high for 2 minutes. Remove the towel and drain off the excess fat, then add the onion and celery to the bowl. Toss the bacon and vegetables together, cover the bowl, and microwave on high for 90 seconds. Stir in the cornflour mixture and the vinegar. Cover the bowl and microwave it on high until the dressing thickens slightly — about 2 minutes.

Cut the potatoes into slices about 5 mm (¼ inch) thick. Pour the dressing over the potato slices; add a generous grinding of pepper and half the parsley. Gently toss the salad, then cool somewhat. Scatter the remaining parsley over the top just before serving.

Vegetable Salad à la Grecque

Serves 8 as a side dish
Working time: about 35 minutes
Total time: about 1 hour

Calories **45**
Protein **2g**
Cholesterol **0mg**
Total fat **2g**
Saturated fat **0g**
Sodium **70mg**

1	leek, trimmed, split, washed thoroughly to remove all grit, and thinly sliced	1
4	garlic cloves, sliced	4
500 g	courgettes, cut into 2.5 cm (1 inch) long cylinders and quartered lengthwise	1 lb
250 g	mushrooms, wiped clean and sliced	8 oz
1	lemon, juice only	1
1	sweet red pepper, seeded, deribbed and cut lengthwise into thin strips	1
1 tsp	chopped fresh thyme, or ¼ tsp dried thyme	1 tsp
½ tsp	chopped fresh rosemary, or ¼ tsp dried rosemary, crumbled	½ tsp
¼ tsp	fennel seeds, crushed	¼ tsp
¼ tsp	salt	¼ tsp
	freshly ground black pepper	
1 tbsp	virgin olive oil	1 tbsp

Place the leek and garlic in a shallow baking dish. Pour in 12.5 cl (4 fl oz) of water and cover the dish with plastic film leaving one end slightly open to allow steam to escape. Microwave the dish on high for 4 minutes, stirring the vegetables after 2 minutes. With a slotted spoon, transfer the leeks and garlic to a large bowl, leaving as much liquid as possible in the dish.

Put the courgettes into the dish, cover it again with plastic film and microwave it on high for 3 minutes. Using the slotted spoon, transfer the courgettes to the bowl containing the leeks.

Place the mushrooms in the dish and pour in the lemon juice; cover once more and cook the mixture on high for 2 minutes. Again using the slotted spoon, transfer the mushrooms to the bowl containing the leek-and-courgette mixture.

Next, stir the pepper strips into the liquid, cover the dish, and cook the pepper strips on high for 2 minutes. Use the slotted spoon to transfer the red pepper to the bowl containing the other vegetables.

Stir the thyme, rosemary and fennel seeds into the liquid remaining in the dish. Cook the liquid, uncovered, on high for 8 minutes, stirring it every 2 minutes. Pour the hot liquid over the vegetables in the bowl, then sprinkle the salt and some pepper over the vegetables. Let the salad marinate until it cools to room temperature — about 30 minutes.

Just before serving, pour the oil over the vegetables and toss the salad well.

Duck and Wild Rice
Salad with
Raspberry Vinaigrette

Serves 6 as a main course at lunch
Working time: about 30 minutes
Total time: about 3 hours and 10 minutes
(includes chilling)

Calories **310**
Protein **25g**
Cholesterol **75mg**
Total fat **12g**
Saturated fat **4g**
Sodium **110mg**

2 kg	duck, rinsed and patted dry	4 lb
5 tbsp	raspberry vinegar	5 tbsp
160 g	wild rice	5½ oz
1	garlic clove, finely chopped	1
100 g	carrot, julienned	3½ oz
120 g	celery, julienned	4 oz
1	large ripe tomato, skinned, seeded and coarsely chopped	1

1 tsp	Dijon mustard	1 tsp
1 tbsp	finely chopped shallot	1 tbsp
	freshly ground black pepper	
3 tbsp	unsalted chicken stock or water	3 tbsp
2 tsp	safflower oil	2 tsp
1	small red-leaf lettuce, washed and dried	1
1	small Batavian endive, washed and dried	1

Trim any excess fat from around the neck of the duck. Remove any fat from the cavity. To release body fat from the duck without rendering its juices as it cooks, lightly prick the duck, taking care not to pierce the flesh below the layer of fat. Using wooden toothpicks, fasten the neck skin to the back of the duck. Sprinkle the inside of the cavity with 1 tablespoon of the vinegar. Place the duck breast side down in a microwave-safe roasting pan and cover it with greaseproof paper. Microwave the duck on medium high (70 per cent power) for 15 minutes. Drain off and discard the fat in the roasting pan. Turn the duck breast side up and cover it with fresh paper. Continue cooking the duck on medium high until the juices run clear when a thigh is pierced with the tip of a sharp knife — about 20 minutes. Drain off and discard the fat, and set the duck aside to cool.

Meanwhile, bring 60 cl (1 pint) of water to the boil in a saucepan. Pour the water into a bowl and add the wild rice and garlic. Cover the bowl and microwave the rice on medium low (30 per cent power) until it is tender — about 30 minutes. Drain the rice, transfer it to a large bowl, and refrigerate it.

Put the carrot and celery julienne into a bowl with 2 tablespoons of hot water. Cover the bowl and microwave the vegetables on high until they are tender — 2 to 3 minutes. Drain the vegetables and combine them with the rice; return the mixture to the refrigerator.

When the duck is cool enough to handle, pull off its skin. Cut the meat from the duck and slice it into thin strips. Toss the strips with the rice-and-vegetable mixture. Stir in the tomato and 2 tablespoons of the remaining vinegar, and set the bowl aside.

In a small bowl, combine the mustard, shallot, some pepper, the remaining vinegar and the stock or water. Whisking vigorously, pour in the oil in a thin, steady stream; continue whisking until the mixture is well combined. Pour the vinaigrette over the duck mixture and toss it well. Chill the salad for about 2 hours to meld its flavours.

To serve the salad, arrange the lettuce and Batavian endive leaves on a serving platter and mound the salad on top of them. Serve immediately.

Wilted Spinach Salad

Serves 4 as a side dish
Working time: about 15 minutes
Total time: about 20 minutes

Calories **95**
Protein **5g**
Cholesterol **0mg**
Total fat **1g**
Saturated fat **0g**
Sodium **200mg**

6 tbsp	rice vinegar	6 tbsp
1 tbsp	sugar	1 tbsp
2 tsp	low-sodium soy sauce or shoyu	2 tsp
2 tsp	sweet chili sauce	2 tsp
2 tbsp	cornflour, mixed with 12.5 cl (4 fl oz) unsalted chicken stock	2 tbsp
250 g	canned straw mushrooms, drained, stem tips cut off, or 300 g (10 oz) fresh mushrooms, wiped clean and stemmed	8 oz
125 g	pearl onions, peeled, blanched in boiling water for 2 minutes	4 oz
500 g	fresh spinach, washed, stemmed, dried and torn into pieces	1 lb
1	sheet nori, crumbled (optional)	1

Combine all of the ingredients except the spinach and nori in a bowl. Stir the mixture well, then microwave it on high until it thickens slightly — about 3 minutes. Thoroughly stir the dressing again, then pour it over the spinach. Toss the spinach to coat it evenly; sprinkle it with the nori if you are using it, and serve the salad at once.

Barley Salad with Orange-Shallot Dressing

Serves 10 as a side dish
Working time: about 25 minutes
Total time: about 1 hour and 15 minutes

Calories **125**
Protein **4g**
Cholesterol **5mg**
Total fat **4g**
Saturated fat **1g**
Sodium **85mg**

200 g	pearl barley	7 oz
4	shallots, finely chopped	4
1	garlic clove, finely chopped	1
1	orange, juice reserved, rind grated	1
60 g	mild back bacon, cut into 5 mm (¼ inch) cubes	2 oz
4 tbsp	chopped parsley	4 tbsp
2 tbsp	safflower oil	2 tbsp
4	ripe tomatoes, sliced	4

Bring 1 litre (1¾ pints) of water to the boil and pour it into a 4 litre (7 pint) bowl. Add the barley, cover the bowl and microwave the barley on high, stirring it every 5 minutes, until it is tender — about 25 minutes. Let the barley stand for at least 10 minutes.

To prepare the dressing, combine the shallots, garlic, orange juice, ½ teaspoon of the grated rind and the bacon in a shallow dish. Cover the dish and microwave the dressing on high for 2 minutes.

Drain the barley and stir in the dressing. Let the salad stand until it cools to room temperature — about 30 minutes. Mix the parsley and oil into the salad, garnish it with the tomato slices, and serve at once.

Moulded Asparagus Timbales

Serves 6 as a first course
Working time: about 30 minutes
Total time: about 6 hours and 30 minutes
(includes chilling)

Calories **60**
Protein **7g**
Cholesterol **2mg**
Total fat **2g**
Saturated fat **1g**
Sodium **110mg**

500 g	medium asparagus, trimmed and peeled	1 lb
¼ litre	cold unsalted chicken stock	8 fl oz
1 tsp	powdered gelatine	1 tsp
125 g	firm tofu	4 oz
100 g	low-fat cottage cheese	3½ oz
12.5 cl	plain low-fat yogurt	4 fl oz
2	spring onions, trimmed and coarsely chopped	2
1	fresh hot green chili pepper, seeded (caution, page 17)	1
3 tbsp	finely cut fresh dill, or 1 tbsp dried dill mixed with 2 tbsp chopped parsley	3 tbsp
	lettuce leaves, washed and dried, for garnish	

Arrange the asparagus spears in a single layer on a dinner plate. Cover the plate tightly with plastic film and microwave the asparagus on high for 2 to 3 minutes, rotating the plate a quarter turn midway through the cooking time. Set the asparagus spears aside but do not uncover them.

Pour the stock into a 60 cl (1 pint) glass measuring jug. Sprinkle the gelatine over the stock and stir it in. Microwave the mixture on high for 4 minutes, then stir it to ensure that the gelatine has dissolved. If it has not, microwave the mixture for 1 minute more.

Purée the tofu, cottage cheese, yogurt, spring onions, chili pepper, and dill or dill-and-parsley mixture in a food processor or blender. Pour the purée into a large bowl and stir in the gelatine mixture. Set the bowl aside.

Cut off and reserve 18 asparagus tips for garnish. Coarsely chop the remaining asparagus and combine it with the gelatine mixture. Divide the mixture evenly between six 12.5 cl (4 fl oz) ramekins. Refrigerate the ramekins until the mixture has set — at least 6 hours.

To serve, run the tip of a knife round the inside of a ramekin to loosen the sides of the timbale. Set the ramekin in a shallow bowl of hot water for 15 seconds to loosen the bottom, then invert the timbale on to a small plate. Repeat the process to unmould the other timbales. Garnish each with three asparagus tips; arrange a few lettuce leaves round the timbale and serve immediately.

THYME

TARRAGON

BASIL

CHERVIL

CHIVES

CORIANDER

A Wealth of Salad Herbs

The 14 herbs depicted here are all called for in this book. Fresh are generally preferred to the dried, both for flavour and colour, but dried herbs may be substituted in most instances and thus the recipes list dried as options wherever appropriate.

Increasingly, herbs are arriving in the markets fresh; the proliferation of health stores and other specialist shops has widened choice. And many cooks with gardens have taken to raising their own. Recent ethnic influences have called attention to once seemingly esoteric herbs. Coriander, for one, is at last gaining deserved popularity in Europe, although cooks in Asia and the Middle East have been using it for centuries.

Anyone wishing to dry fresh herbs can tie them loosely in a bundle and hang them upside down in a cool, dark, well-ventilated place for several weeks. When the leaves are completely dried, strip them from the stems and store them in an airtight container.

Two swifter methods of preserving herbs make use of the microwave oven and the freezer. To microwave herbs, place five or six sprigs at a time between paper towels and microwave them on high for 1 to 3 minutes until the leaves are brittle. Store the leaves loosely in airtight jars.

To freeze herbs, rinse the sprigs and pat them dry. Strip the leaves off the stems and put them into a heavy-duty plastic bag. Gently flatten the bag to force out the air, seal the bag tightly, and place it in your freezer. Use the leaves as the need arises.

Basil (also called sweet basil): This fragrant herb, with its underlying flavour of anise and hint of clove, goes particularly well with tomato.

Chervil: The small, lacy leaves of this herb have a taste akin to parsley with a touch of anise. It is good in salads and salad dressings. Chervil is popular in France where it is often an ingredient in herb mixtures, including *fines herbes*. When used in cooking, chervil should be added at the end, lest its subtle flavour be lost.

Chives: The smallest of the onions, chives grow in grassy clumps. When finely cut, the hollow leaves contribute their delicate, oniony flavour to fresh salads and raw vegetables. Chives should always be used fresh, as dried ones are virtually tasteless.

Coriander (also called cilantro): The serrated leaves of the coriander plant impart a distinctive fragrance and a flavour that is both mildly sweet and bitter. Coriander leaves should be used fresh or added at the end of cooking if their flavour is to be appreciated fully.

Dill: A sprightly herb with feathery leaves, dill enhances cucumber and many other fresh vegetables, as well as fish and shellfish. When used in cooking, dill should be added towards the end of the process to preserve its delicate flavour. Both dill

ROSEMARY

SAGE

PARSLEY, FLAT-LEAF

PARSLEY, CURLY

OREGANO

seeds and dill leaves can be steeped for several weeks in a bottle of white, cider or white wine vinegar to make a herb vinegar.

Marjoram (also called sweet marjoram): A native of the Mediterranean, this perfumed herb has tender, small green leaves. The flavour is similar to that of oregano, only more subtle. Whole leaves may be used to flavour salads; they can also be added fresh or dried to salad dressings.

Mint: Of this large family of herbs, the most common variety is spearmint, illustrated here. Spearmint leaves, with serrated edges and pebbly surfaces, have a sweeter taste than peppermint. They contribute a refreshing sparkle to salads; spearmint sprigs make attractive garnishes.

Oregano: This robust, strong-smelling herb with a trace of bitterness lends character to both salads and salad dressings. A close relative of marjoram, oregano has leaves that are generally larger and more pointed. The flavour of the leaves intensifies when oregano is dried.

Parsley, curly: The most common fresh herb on the market, clean-tasting curly parsley is widely used to garnish salads but also has enough character in its own right to be an integral part of many salad preparations.

Parsley, flat-leaf: A relative of the popular curly parsley, flat-leaf parsley has straight, broad leaves and is preferred by many cooks because its flavour is more distinct than that of curly parsley.

Rosemary: A rich-smelling herb, with an almost piney aroma, this native of the Mediterranean grows as a shrubby evergreen. Like oregano, sage and thyme, rosemary retains much of its flavour after drying and stays potent through cooking. It is often paired with roasted and grilled meats, especially lamb.

Sage: The resin-scented, greyish-green leaves have a hint of bitterness and of camphor. Chopped, they may be added to salads, poultry stuffings and pork. Dried, they not only retain much of their flavour, but a pleasant muskiness emerges.

Tarragon: A delightful anise flavour permeates the leaves of this herb. The French variety is preferred. A tarragon-flavoured vinegar can readily be made by steeping whole sprigs of the herb in a bottle of vinegar for several weeks; the sprigs may be left in the bottle.

Thyme: The tiny leaves of this herb pack an abundance of earthy flavour. Thyme can be added fresh or dried to salads, dressings and vinegars. It is an essential component in a *bouquet garni*, along with parsley and bay leaf. Thyme leaves dry well.

MARJORAM

DILL

MINT

Glossary

Al dente: an Italian term meaning "to the tooth". It is used to describe the texture and taste of perfectly cooked pasta: chewy but with no flavour of flour.

Almond oil: a highly fragrant oil used in small amounts to flavour salads. Its traditional role is as a flavouring agent in confectionery.

Arugula: see Rocket, page 8.

Balsamic vinegar: a mild, intensely fragrant wine-based vinegar made in northern Italy; traditionally it is aged in wooden casks.

Basil: see page 138.

Batavian endive: see page 9.

Bâtonnet: French for "little stick". Used to describe the size and shape of vegetables cut into pieces about 4 cm (1½ inches) long and 5 mm (¼ inch) square.

Beet greens: the tops of beetroot, sometimes sold separately, eaten as a nutritious green vegetable. Certain varieties are grown as much for their tops as for their roots. See also page 8.

Black vinegar, Chinese (also called Chenkong vinegar, Chinkiang vinegar): a dark vinegar made from fermented rice.

Blanch: to partially cook food by immersing it briefly in boiling water.

Broad beans: a European variety of bean with large seeds and thick pods, eaten fresh or dried. Except for the very youngest broad beans, only the seeds are edible and the maturer ones should also have their thin skins removed before cooking.

Buckwheat: the seed of the flowering buckwheat plant. Buckwheat groats (also called kasha) are hulled, steamed, dried and sometimes toasted to intensify flavour. Buckwheat flour is unrelated to wheat flour and lacks the proteins required to form gluten.

Bulb fennel: see Fennel.

Burghul: (also called bulgur): a type of cracked wheat, where the kernels are steamed and dried before being crushed.

Calorie (or kilocalorie): a precise measure of the energy food supplies when it is broken down for use in the body.

Capers: the pickled flower buds of the caper plant, a shrub native to the Mediterranean. Capers should be rinsed before use to rid them of excess salt.

Cardamom: the bittersweet, aromatic dried seeds or whole pods of a plant in the ginger family. Cardamom seeds may be used whole or ground.

Celeriac (also called celery root): the knobby, tuberous root of a plant in the celery family.

Ceps (also called porcini): wild mushrooms with a pungent, earthy flavour that survives drying or long cooking. Dried ceps should be soaked in water before they are used.

Chayote (also called christophine): a pear-shaped, pale green squash that remains crisp when cooked.

Chervil: see page 138.

Chicory: see page 8.

Chili paste: a robust, spicy paste made from chili peppers, salt and other ingredients. Numerous kinds are available in Asian shops.

Chili peppers: hot or mild red, yellow or green members of the pepper family. Fresh or dried, most chili peppers contain volatile oils that can irritate the skin and eyes; they must be handled with extreme care *(caution, page 17).*

Chinese black vinegar: see Black vinegar, Chinese.

Chinese cabbage (also called Chinese leaves): an elongated cabbage resembling cos lettuce, with long broad ribs and crinkled, light green to white leaves. See also page 10.

Chives: see page 138.

Cholesterol: a wax-like substance manufactured in the human body and also found in foods of animal origin. Although a certain amount of cholesterol is necessary for proper body functioning, an excess can accumulate in the arteries, contributing to heart disease. See also Monounsaturated fats; Polyunsaturated fats; Saturated fats.

Cilantro: see Coriander.

Coriander (also called cilantro): the pungent, peppery leaves of the coriander plant or its earthy tasting dried seeds. It is a common seasoning in Middle-Eastern, Oriental and Latin-American cookery. See also page 138.

Corn salad: see Lamb's lettuce, page 9.

Couscous: cereal processed from semolina into pellets, traditionally steamed and served with meat and vegetables in the classic North African stew of the same name.

Crystallized ginger (also called candied ginger): stems of ginger preserved with sugar. Crystallized ginger should not be confused with ginger in syrup.

Cumin: the aromatic seeds of an umbelliferous plant similar to fennel used, whole or powdered, as a spice, especially in Indian and Latin-American dishes. Toasting gives it a nutty flavour.

Curly endive: see page 8.

Daikon radish (also called mooli): a long, white Japanese radish.

Dandelion greens: these, like nettles, make a delicious salad ingredient. Pick the leaves in spring before the flowers appear. The darker leaves that develop in summer tend to have a bitter taste. See also page 9.

Dark sesame oil: a dark seasoning oil, high in polyunsaturated fats, that is made from toasted sesame seeds. Because dark sesame oil has a relatively low smoking point, it is rarely heated. Dark sesame oil should not be confused or replaced with lighter sesame cooking oils.

Debeard: to remove the fibrous threads from a mussel. These threads, called the beard, are produced by the mussel to attach itself to stationary objects.

Devein: to remove the intestinal vein that runs along the outer curve of a prawn. To devein a prawn, peel it first, then make a shallow cut along the line of the vein and scrape out the vein with the tip of the knife.

Dijon mustard: a smooth mustard once manufactured only in Dijon, France; it may be flavoured with herbs, green peppercorns or wine.

Dill: see page 138.

Ditalini: a short, dried tubular pasta.

Escarole: see Batavian endive, page 9.

Fennel: a herb (also called wild fennel) whose feathery leaves and dried seeds have a mild anise flavour and are much used for flavouring. Its vegetable relative, the bulb — or Florence — fennel (also called finocchio) can be cooked, or eaten raw in salads.

Fermented black beans: soya beans that have been fermented, dried and salted. Fermented black beans should be rinsed before use to rid them of excess salt.

Five-spice powder: a pungent blend of ground Sichuan pepper, star anise, cassia, cloves and fennel seeds; available in Asian food shops.

Garter beans: a variety of green bean that averages 30 cm (1 ft) in length. More tender than standard green beans, they are available in Asian food shops.

Ginger: the spicy, buff-coloured rhizome, or rootlike stem, of the ginger plant, used as a seasoning either in fresh form or dried and powdered. Dried ginger makes a poor substitute for fresh ginger root. See also Crystallized ginger.

Hoisin sauce: a thick, dark reddish-brown sauce made from soya beans, flour, garlic, sugar and spices.

Jerusalem artichoke: neither from Jerusalem nor an artichoke, this vegetable is the tuberous root of a member of the sunflower family. In texture, colour and flavour it resembles the water chestnut.

Julienne: the French term for vegetables or other food cut into strips.

Kale: see page 9.

Kasha: see Buckwheat groats.

Kohlrabi: a cruciferous vegetable with an enlarged stem in the form of a light-green or lavender bulb.

Lamb's lettuce: see page 9.

Mâche: see Lamb's lettuce, page 9.

Mange-tout: flat green pea pods eaten whole, with only stems and strings removed.

Marjoram: see page 139.

Millet: a nutritious grain with a nutty, mild taste.

Mint: see page 139.

Mirin: a sweet Japanese cooking wine made from rice. If mirin is unavailable, substitute white wine or sake mixed with a little sugar.

Monkfish (also called angler-fish): an Atlantic fish with a scaleless, thick-skinned body and an enormous ugly head; only the tail portion, however, is edible. Its lean, firm, somewhat dry flesh is thought by some to resemble lobster in flavour.

Monounsaturated fats: one of the three types of fats found in foods. Monounsaturated fats are believed not to raise the level of cholesterol in the blood.

Mustard greens (also called green-in-snow, Chinese mustard): this nutritious member of the brassica family is a popular vegetable in the U.S. It is not yet widely available in Europe, though increasingly grown by home gardeners from seed. See also page 10.

Non-reactive pan: a cooking vessel whose surface does not chemically react with food. Materials used include stainless steel, enamel, glass and some alloys. Untreated cast iron and aluminium may react with acids, producing discoloration or a peculiar taste.

Nori: paper-like dark green or black sheets of dried seaweed, often used in Japanese cuisine as a flavouring or as wrappers for rice and vegetables.

Oakleaf lettuce: see page 10.

Olive oil: any of various grades of oil extracted from olives. Extra virgin olive oil has a full, fruity flavour and very low acidity. Virgin olive oil is lighter in flavour and slightly higher in acidity. Pure olive oil, a processed blend of olive oils, has the lightest taste and highest acidity. For salad dressings, virgin and extra virgin olive oils are preferred. Store in a cool, dark place.

Orzo: a rice-shaped dried pasta.
Pancetta: a salted — not smoked — Italian bacon, available at Italian delicatessens.
Parsley: see page 139.
Penne: a tubular dried pasta with diagonally cut ends. The word is Italian for "pens" or "quills".
Pine-nuts: seeds from the cone of the stone pine, a tree native to the Mediterranean. Pine-nuts are used in pesto and other sauces; their buttery flavour can be heightened by light toasting.
Polenta: cooked cornmeal, traditionally eaten in northern Italy.
Polyunsaturated fats: one of the three types of fat found in foods. They exist in abundance in such vegetable oils as safflower, sunflower, corn and soya bean. Polyunsaturated fats lower the level of cholesterol in the blood.
Radicchio: see page 11.
Recommended daily amount (RDA): the average daily amount of an essential nutrient recommended for healthy people by the U.K. Department of Health and Social Security.
Red chicory: see Radicchio, page 11.
Reduce: to boil down a liquid in order to concentrate its flavour and thicken its consistency.
Refresh: to rinse a briefly cooked vegetable under cold water to arrest its cooking and set its colour.
Rice vinegar: a mild, fragrant vinegar that is less assertive than cider vinegar or distilled white vinegar. It is available in dark, light, seasoned and sweetened varieties; Japanese rice vinegar generally is milder than the Chinese version.
Rocket: see page 8.
Rosemary: see page 139.
Safflower oil: a vegetable oil that contains a high proportion of polyunsaturated fats.
Saffron: the dried, yellowish-red stigmas (or threads) of the saffron crocus, which yield a powerful yellow colour as well as a pungent flavour. Powdered saffron may be substituted for the threads but has less flavour.
Sage: see page 139.
Saturated fats: one of the three types of fat found in foods. They exist in abundance in animal products and coconut and palm oils; they raise the level of cholesterol in the blood. Because high blood-cholesterol levels may cause heart disease, saturated

fat consumption should be restricted to less than 15 per cent of the calories provided by the daily diet.
Sauté: to cook a food quickly in a small amount of oil or butter over high heat.
Savoy cabbage: see page 11.
Sesame oil: see Dark sesame oil.
Sesame paste: see Tahini.
Seviche (ceviche): originally, a Peruvian dish made of raw white fish or scallops combined with lemon or lime juice, onion, hot red pepper flakes and black peppercorns. The term is now often used for any dish in which fish or shellfish marinates in citrus juice.
Sherry vinegar: a full-bodied vinegar made from sherry; its distinguishing feature is a sweet aftertaste.
Shiitake mushrooms: a variety of mushroom, originally grown only in Japan, sold fresh or dried. The dried form should be soaked and stemmed before use.
Sichuan pepper (also called anise pepper, Chinese pepper and Japanese pepper): the dried berry of a shrub native to China. Its flavour is tart and aromatic, but less piquant than that of black pepper.
Sodium: a nutrient essential to maintaining the proper balance of fluids in the body. In most diets, a major source of the element is table salt, made up of 40 per cent sodium. Excess sodium may contribute to high blood pressure, which increases the risk of heart disease. One teaspoon (5.5 g) of salt, with 2,132 milligrams of sodium, contains just over the maximum daily amount recommended by the World Health Organization.
Sorrel: see page 11.
Soy sauce: a savoury, salty brown liquid made from fermented soya beans and available in both light and dark versions. One tablespoon of ordinary soy sauce contains 1,030 milligrams of sodium; lower-sodium variations, such as naturally fermented shoyu, may contain half that amount.
Soya bean paste (or bean sauce): a thick brown paste made from soya beans, spices and salt.
Stock: a savoury liquid, most often used as a flavour-rich base for sauces, that is made by simmering aromatic vegetables, herbs, spices, bones and meat trimmings in water. Unsalted, defatted chicken or veal stock is often used to enrich the dressings in this book without adding unwanted fat.
Straw mushrooms: cultivated mushrooms with

pointed caps and a silky texture. Straw mushrooms are usually available in either cans or jars.
Sugar snap peas: a variation of garden pea; when stem and string are removed, the entire pod may be eaten.
Sun-dried tomatoes: tomatoes that have been dried in the open air to concentrate their flavour; some are then packed in oil. Most sun-dried tomatoes are of Italian origin.
Tahini (also called sesame paste): a nutty-tasting paste made from ground sesame seeds that are usually roasted.
Tarragon: see page 139.
Thyme: see page 139.
Tofu (also called bean curd): a dense, soya bean product with a mild flavour. Tofu is rich in protein, relatively low in calories and free of cholesterol. It is highly perishable and should be kept refrigerated, submerged in water; if the water is changed daily, the tofu may be stored for up to a week.
Total fat: an individual's daily intake of polyunsaturated, monounsaturated and saturated fats. Nutritionists recommend that fats constitute no more than 35 per cent of a person's total calorie intake. The term as used in the nutrient analyses in this book refers to all the sources of fat in a recipe.
Virgin olive oil: see Olive oil.
Walnut oil: an oil extracted from pressed walnuts. Its distinctive flavour adds balance to such bitter greens as curly endive. It should be purchased in small quantities; once opened, it can turn rancid within just a few weeks.
Water chestnut: the walnut-sized tuber of an aquatic Asian plant, with rough brown skin and white, sweet, crisp flesh. Fresh water chestnuts may be refrigerated for up to two weeks; they must be peeled before use. To store canned water chestnuts, first blanch or rinse them, then refrigerate for up to three weeks in fresh water changed daily. Jerusalem artichoke makes an acceptable substitute.
Watercress: see page 11.
Wheat berries: unpolished, whole-wheat kernels with a nutty taste and chewy texture.
Wild rice: the seeds of a water grass native to the Great Lakes region of the United States. Wild rice is appreciated for its robust flavour.
Ziti: dried tubular pasta about 4 cm (1½ inches) long.

Index

Picture Credits

All photographs in this book were taken by staff photographer Renée Comet unless otherwise indicated:

Cover: James Murphy. 2: top and centre, Carolyn Wall Rothery. 5: left, Steven Biver; right, Michael Latil. 8-11: Michael Latil. 16, 17: Taran Z. 19: top, John Elliott. 32: top, John Elliott. 34: Michael Latil. 37: Taran Z. 40: Michael Geiger. 43: top, Taran Z. 44: bottom, Michael Latil. 45: Michael Latil. 47: top, Michael Latil. 50: Taran Z. 51: left, Taran Z. 55: Taran Z. 57: top, Michael Latil. 60: Taran Z. 62: Michael Latil. 63: Taran Z. 66: Michael Latil. 67: Steven Biver. 68-70: Michael Latil. 72: Taran Z. 73: Steven Biver. 77: Michael Latil. 78, 79: Steven Biver. 81: Michael Latil. 82: Steven Biver. 85, 86: Michael Latil. 88: Michael Latil. 90: Michael Latil. 91: Steven Biver. 93: Michael Latil. 96: Michael Ward. 99: Michael Ward. 105, 106: Steven Biver. 109: Steven Biver. 110: top, Michael Ward. 112: Steven Biver. 113: right, Michael Ward. 114: Michael Geiger. 115: Michael Latil. 117: top, John Elliott; bottom, Michael Latil. 118: Michael Latil. 120: Steven Biver. 121: Michael Latil. 124: Michael Latil. 125: Steven Biver. 130: Michael Ward. 132: Michael Ward. 133: Michael Latil. 134-136: Michael Ward. 137: Michael Latil. 138, 139: Taran Z.

Acknowledgements

The editors are particularly indebted to the following people: Leslie Bloom, Silver Spring, Md., U.S.A.; Nora Carey, Paris; Carole Clements, Paris; Sharon Farrington, Bethesda, Md., U.S.A.; Carol Gvozdich, Alexandria, Va., U.S.A.; Maggie Heinz, London; Michael Krondl, New York; Nancy Lendved, Alexandria, Va., U.S.A.; Shahnaz Mehta, McLean, Va., U.S.A.; Ann Ready, Alexandria, Va., U.S.A.; Tina Ujlaki, New York; Rita Walters, London; Sarah Wiley, London.

The editors also wish to thank: Jo Calabrese, Royal Worcester Spode Inc., New York; Jackie Chalkley, Fine Crafts and Wearables, Washington, D.C.; Nic Colling, Home Produce Company, Alexandria, Va., U.S.A.; Margaret Berry Cotton, Hanover, N.H., U.S.A.; Cuisinarts, Inc., Greenwich, Conn., U.S.A.; Jeanne Dale, The Pilgrim Glass Corp., New York; Rex Downey, Oxon Hill, Md., U.S.A.; Flowers Unique, Alexandria, Va., U.S.A.; Flying Foods, International, Long Island City, N.Y., U.S.A.; Dennis Garrett, Ed Nash, The American Hand Plus, Washington, D.C.; Giant Foods, Inc., Landover, Md., U.S.A.; Judith Goodkind, Alexandria, Va., U.S.A.; Chong Su Han, Grass Roots Restaurant, Alexandria, Va., U.S.A.; Ken Hancock, Annandale, Va., U.S.A.; Joe Huffer, Mount Solon, Va., U.S.A.; Imperial Produce, Washington, D.C.; Kitchen Bazaar, Washington , D.C.; KitchenAid, Inc., Troy, Ohio, U.S.A.; Kossow Gourmet Produce, Washington, D.C.; Gary Latzman, Kirk Phillips, Retroneu, New York; Magruder's, Inc., Rockville, Md., U.S.A.; Sara Mark, Alexandria, Va., U.S.A.; Nambé Mills Inc., Sante Fe, N. Mex., U.S.A.; Andrew Naylor, Alexandria, Va., U.S.A.; Hiu Newcomb, Potomac Vegetable Farms, Vienna, Va., U.S.A.; Oster, Milwaukee, Wis., U.S.A.; Lisa Ownby, Alexandria, Va., U.S.A.; Joyce Piotrowski, Vienna, Va., U.S.A.; RT's Restaurant, Alexandria, Va., U.S.A.; Linda Robertson, JUD Tile, Vienna, Va., U.S.A.; Safeway Stores, Inc., Landover, Md., U.S.A.; Bert Saunders, WILTON Armetale, New York; Schiller & Asmus, Inc., Yemasse, S.C., U.S.A.; Nancy Snyder, Snyder's Sprouts, Rockville, Md., U.S.A.; Straight from the Crate, Inc., Alexandria, Va., U.S.A.; Sutton Place Gourmet, Washington, D.C.; Kathy Swekel, Columbia, Md., U.S.A.; Nancy Teksten, National Onion Association, Greeley, Colorado, U.S.A.; 219 Restaurant, Alexandria, Va., U.S.A.; U.S. Fish, Kensington, Md., U.S.A.; Williams-Sonoma, Washington, D.C.; Lynn Addison Yorke, Cheverly, Md., U.S.A.

Typesetting by G. Beard & Sons Ltd., Brighton, Sussex, England.
Printed and bound by Oriental Press, Dubai.